Bug Bounty Unleashed

Mastering the Art of Ethical Hacking and Rewards

Russell Yates

In an ever-evolving digital landscape, the battle between cybersecurity defenders and malicious actors continues to intensify. As technology advances and online assets become more crucial, organizations face an ever-increasing risk of cyber threats that can lead to severe consequences—financial losses, data breaches, reputational damage, and even the compromise of critical infrastructures.

In this age of constant digital peril, ethical hacking has emerged as a powerful weapon in the fight against cyber threats. Bug bounty programs, at the forefront of ethical hacking initiatives, have revolutionized the way vulnerabilities are identified and mitigated. By harnessing the collective power of ethical hackers worldwide, these programs have enabled organizations to fortify their defenses proactively.

Welcome to **"<u>Bug Bounty Unleashed: Mastering the Art of Ethical Hacking and Rewards</u>."** This book serves as your comprehensive guide to exploring the exhilarating world of ethical hacking and bug bounty hunting. Whether you are an aspiring ethical hacker, a seasoned cybersecurity professional, or simply an individual intrigued by the realm of digital security, this book will equip you with the knowledge and skills to become a proficient bug bounty hunter.

Chapter by Chapter, Unleashing Your Potential

Throughout this book, we will delve into the intricacies of ethical hacking, bug bounty hunting, and the methodologies behind securing digital systems. From foundational concepts to advanced techniques, we will take you on a journey that encompasses both theoretical principles and practical hands-on experience.

In Chapter 1, **"Introduction to Bug Bounty Hunting,"** we will lay the groundwork by exploring the essence of bug bounty programs, their significance in the cybersecurity landscape, and the rewarding experiences they offer.

Chapter 2, **"Preparing for Bug Bounty Hunting,"** will focus on the fundamental knowledge and skills you need to possess as a bug bounty hunter. From understanding the cybersecurity landscape to setting up a secure testing environment, you will be primed for the challenges ahead.

Next, in Chapter 3, **"Ethical Hacking Methodology,"** we will unravel the hacker's mindset and delve into the steps involved in uncovering vulnerabilities ethically. We will guide you through the crucial stages of reconnaissance, vulnerability assessment, and exploitation.

In Chapter 4, **"Types of Vulnerabilities and Exploits,"** we will examine common security flaws present in web applications, networks, and mobile environments. You will gain a deep understanding of these vulnerabilities and the methods used to exploit them.

As you venture further into the world of bug bounty hunting, Chapter 5, **"Bug Bounty Platforms and Strategies,"** will introduce you to the various platforms that host bug bounty programs. Additionally, we will provide you with strategies to optimize your bug hunting endeavors.

A crucial aspect of bug bounty hunting is the process of **"Reporting Bugs Effectively,"** which will be explored in Chapter 6. Here, you will learn the art of crafting comprehensive bug reports, communicating with program owners, and ensuring responsible disclosure.

As you navigate the ethical hacking landscape, Chapter 7, **"Responsible Disclosure and Legal Considerations,"** will shed light on the ethical and legal responsibilities of bug bounty hunters. You will gain insights into the best practices for disclosure and the potential legal implications of your actions.

In Chapter 8, **"Challenges and Lessons from Real-Life Bug Bounties,"** we will present case studies and experiences of successful bug hunters. By analyzing both achievements and setbacks, you will learn invaluable lessons that will propel your journey as an ethical hacker.

As technology advances, so do the battlegrounds of cyber threats. Chapter 9, **"Bug Bounty Hunting in IoT and OT Environments,"** will delve into the unique challenges and vulnerabilities present in the realm of the Internet of Things (IoT) and Operational Technology (OT).

Chapter 10, **"Bug Bounty Hunting in Cloud and Containerized Environments,"** will explore security considerations for cloud-based services and containerized applications, which have become essential components of modern-day infrastructures.

In Chapter 11, **"Maximizing Bug Bounty Rewards and Recognition,"** we will equip you with the skills to negotiate bounties effectively, establish your reputation in the bug bounty community, and gain the recognition you deserve.

Finally, in Chapter 12, **"The Future of Bug Bounty Hunting,"** we will peer into the horizon of cybersecurity's future. Emerging trends, challenges, and the integration of artificial intelligence in ethical hacking will be among the topics we discuss.

Your Ethical Hacking Journey Begins Now

With "Bug Bounty Unleashed: Mastering the Art of Ethical Hacking and Rewards" as your guide, you will embark on an exciting and impactful journey as an ethical hacker. Throughout this book, we encourage you to embrace the spirit of ethical hacking, to think outside the box, and to contribute to a safer digital world.

So, let the bug bounty be unleashed, and let your passion for cybersecurity propel you towards mastering the art of ethical hacking and the rewards it brings!

Happy hunting!

Russell Yates

Chapter 1: Introduction to Bug Bounty Hunting

In an era where cybersecurity breaches and data compromises have become all too common, the need for a proactive and robust defense against malicious hackers is greater than ever before. Amidst this digital battleground, a new breed of warriors has emerged—ethical hackers.

Welcome to Chapter 1 of "Bug Bounty Unleashed: Mastering the Art of Ethical Hacking and Rewards." In this chapter, we embark on an exciting journey into the world of bug bounty hunting—a thrilling and rewarding pursuit that leverages the power of ethical hacking to bolster cybersecurity defenses.

A New Era in Cybersecurity

Gone are the days when security vulnerabilities were considered a hidden menace. Bug bounty hunting has revolutionized the way organizations approach cybersecurity by harnessing the collective intelligence of ethical hackers from around the globe. In this collaborative landscape, defenders and hackers unite with a shared purpose—to identify and rectify vulnerabilities before malicious actors can exploit them.

Understanding Bug Bounty Programs

In this chapter, we lay the foundation by exploring the essence of bug bounty programs. You will gain a comprehensive understanding of what these programs entail, how they function, and the significant role they play in fortifying digital assets. We will examine the various types of bug bounty programs and the industries that have embraced this innovative approach to security.

Embracing the Spirit of Ethical Hacking

To be a successful bug bounty hunter, one must embrace the ethos of ethical hacking. Throughout this chapter, we will delve into the principles and values that underpin the ethical hacker's mindset. Understanding the distinction between ethical hacking and malicious activities is vital as you embark on your bug bounty hunting journey.

Unleashing the Rewards

Bug bounty hunting is not merely a noble pursuit; it also offers enticing rewards. In this chapter, we explore the incentives that entice ethical hackers to participate in bug bounty programs. From financial bounties to recognition within the cybersecurity community, you will discover the diverse array of rewards awaiting skilled hunters.

Equipping Yourself for the Journey

As we conclude this introductory chapter, we will provide you with practical advice on preparing yourself to embark on a bug bounty hunting adventure. Building a solid foundation of cybersecurity knowledge and mastering key technical skills will empower you to tackle the challenges that lie ahead with confidence.

Are you ready to venture into the thrilling world of bug bounty hunting? Join us as we unravel the mysteries of ethical hacking, explore vulnerabilities, and discover the secrets of securing digital landscapes one bug at a time. Let us embrace the challenge together, as we master the art of ethical hacking and uncover the bountiful rewards that await.

1.1 What is Bug Bounty Hunting?

Bug bounty hunting is a dynamic and rewarding field in the realm of cybersecurity, where skilled ethical hackers, also known as bug hunters, collaborate with organizations to identify and responsibly disclose vulnerabilities in their digital systems. This practice aims to bolster the security of software applications, websites, networks, and other technological assets, ultimately enhancing the overall cybersecurity posture of organizations and protecting users from potential threats.

In essence, bug bounty hunting revolves around the concept of incentivized vulnerability discovery. Instead of maliciously exploiting security flaws for personal gain, ethical hackers actively seek out vulnerabilities in a controlled and responsible manner. They then report their findings to the organization or platform that hosts the bug bounty program, allowing them to fix the issues before malicious actors can exploit them.

1.1.1 A Historical Overview

The origins of bug bounty hunting can be traced back to the late 20th century, with notable early examples like Netscape's "Bugs Bounty Program" in 1995. However, it wasn't until the 21st century that bug bounty hunting gained significant traction. Technology giants such as Google and Facebook launched their own bug bounty programs, offering financial rewards to ethical hackers who identified and reported vulnerabilities. These initiatives proved highly successful, inspiring a multitude of other organizations to follow suit.

1.1.2 How Bug Bounty Programs Operate

Bug bounty programs are typically hosted by organizations, software vendors, technology platforms, or even government entities seeking to bolster their cybersecurity defenses. These programs define the scope of what systems, applications, or technologies are eligible for testing, as well as the types of vulnerabilities they are interested in receiving reports about.

Ethical hackers, often referred to as bug hunters or security researchers, participate in these bug bounty programs voluntarily. They explore the defined scope, searching for potential vulnerabilities, and once they discover a security flaw, they report their findings to the program owners through a responsible disclosure process.

1.1.3 Responsible Disclosure and the Role of Ethical Hacking

Responsible disclosure is a critical aspect of bug bounty hunting. It involves a structured and controlled process through which ethical hackers communicate their findings to the organization in question without causing harm or exposing sensitive data. This responsible approach allows the organization to remediate the issue before malicious actors can exploit it.

The role of ethical hacking is pivotal in bug bounty hunting. Ethical hackers, often possessing a deep understanding of various technologies and security principles, apply their expertise to think like malicious actors. They conduct controlled security assessments, testing for potential weaknesses and vulnerabilities that could be exploited by cybercriminals.

1.1.4 Incentives for Bug Hunters

Bug bounty programs offer various incentives to motivate ethical hackers to participate actively. The primary reward is monetary compensation, often provided as a bounty or financial reward for each reported vulnerability. The value of the bounty typically depends on the severity and impact of the discovered vulnerability. Critical vulnerabilities may fetch substantial rewards, reflecting their potential to cause significant harm.

Apart from monetary compensation, ethical hackers may also receive recognition for their contributions. Many organizations publicly acknowledge the efforts of bug hunters through hall of fame listings, certificates, or even job opportunities. This recognition boosts the reputation of ethical hackers within the cybersecurity community and can open doors to lucrative careers in the field.

1.1.5 The Impact and Benefits of Bug Bounty Hunting

Bug bounty hunting offers numerous benefits for organizations, bug hunters, and end-users. For organizations, it represents a cost-effective approach to bolstering security by tapping into the collective expertise of the cybersecurity community. It helps identify and fix vulnerabilities that traditional internal testing might overlook, thus enhancing overall resilience against cyber threats.

For bug hunters, bug bounty programs provide a legitimate and ethical outlet for their hacking skills. They can earn a substantial income while contributing positively to cybersecurity. Additionally, participation in bug bounty programs offers opportunities to enhance technical skills, gain practical experience, and establish a reputation within the cybersecurity community.

End-users also benefit from bug bounty hunting. By proactively identifying and addressing vulnerabilities, organizations can protect user data and prevent potential data breaches or other security incidents. Ultimately, this helps to create a safer digital ecosystem for everyone.

1.1.6 Challenges and Future Developments

Despite its numerous benefits, bug bounty hunting also faces some challenges. One of the main challenges is the potential for duplicate submissions, where multiple bug hunters report the same vulnerability. Properly managing and rewarding these duplicate reports can be complex for organizations.

Another challenge lies in the sheer scale of bug bounty programs, particularly those hosted by large organizations. Handling the influx of submissions, prioritizing and verifying their validity, and providing timely responses to bug hunters can strain the program's resources.

Looking into the future, bug bounty hunting is expected to continue evolving as technology advances. Emerging technologies, such as IoT, cloud computing, and blockchain, will present new challenges and opportunities for bug hunters to uncover vulnerabilities in these cutting-edge domains.

Additionally, the integration of artificial intelligence and automation in bug hunting tools and methodologies will revolutionize the field. AI-driven vulnerability scanning and pattern recognition will enhance the efficiency of bug hunters, allowing them to uncover vulnerabilities at a scale never seen before.

Moreover, as bug bounty hunting becomes more prevalent across various sectors, including critical infrastructures, government agencies, and non-profit organizations, global collaboration will play an increasingly significant role in securing the digital world.

In conclusion, bug bounty hunting plays a vital role in modern cybersecurity efforts, providing a symbiotic relationship between organizations seeking to fortify their defenses and ethical hackers eager to contribute positively to cybersecurity. This cooperative approach to security fosters a safer digital environment for users worldwide and offers an exciting and promising future for the bug bounty hunting community.

1.2 The Evolution of Ethical Hacking

Ethical hacking, also known as penetration testing or white-hat hacking, has evolved significantly since its inception in the 1960s. Initially, it was an informal and ad-hoc practice, but over time, it has grown into a structured and professional field dedicated to securing digital systems and safeguarding data. Let's explore the key milestones in the evolution of ethical hacking:

1.2.1 Early Beginnings and Informal Practices

In the early days of computing, the concept of hacking emerged as enthusiasts explored the limits of computer systems and networks. The term "hacker" originally referred to individuals who had a deep curiosity about technology and sought to understand its inner workings. During this period, hacking was mostly benign, and the motivation was driven by curiosity rather than malicious intent.

1.2.2 Ethical Hacking as a Security Practice

As technology advanced, it became apparent that vulnerabilities in computer systems and networks could be exploited by malicious actors for nefarious purposes. The rise of cyberattacks and the potential consequences of data breaches highlighted the need for a proactive approach to cybersecurity. This realization paved the way for ethical hacking as a security practice.

1.2.3 The Birth of Formal Ethical Hacking Programs

In the 1970s and 1980s, some organizations recognized the value of employing hackers to assess their systems' security. The term "ethical hacking" started gaining traction as a formal practice, and the first ethical hacking programs emerged. Organizations hired skilled hackers to identify weaknesses in their systems, providing valuable feedback for improving security measures.

1.2.4 Hacking Guidelines and Standards

As ethical hacking gained legitimacy, organizations and industry experts began developing guidelines and standards for conducting ethical hacking assessments. One of the notable early frameworks was the Trusted Computer System Evaluation Criteria (TCSEC), also known as the Orange Book, which was published by the U.S. Department of Defense in the 1980s.

1.2.5 Certification Programs for Ethical Hackers

To further professionalize the field of ethical hacking, certification programs were introduced. These programs validated the skills and knowledge of ethical hackers, providing formal recognition for their expertise. The Certified Ethical Hacker (CEH) certification, launched by EC-Council in 2003, became one of the most recognized certifications in the field.

1.2.6 Bug Bounty Programs and Responsible Disclosure

The advent of bug bounty programs in the 2000s revolutionized ethical hacking. Technology companies such as Mozilla, Google, and Facebook started offering financial rewards to ethical hackers who responsibly disclosed vulnerabilities. Bug bounty programs provided a legitimate channel for ethical hackers to contribute to cybersecurity while earning rewards for their efforts.

1.2.7 Collaboration and Global Ethical Hacking Communities

The rise of the internet and online forums facilitated collaboration among ethical hackers worldwide. The emergence of global ethical hacking communities allowed individuals to share knowledge, exchange experiences, and contribute to the collective effort of securing cyberspace. Online platforms such as Bugcrowd and HackerOne became popular hubs for bug bounty hunters and program owners to connect.

1.2.8 Advanced Ethical Hacking Techniques

As technology continued to advance, so did the techniques and tools used by ethical hackers. Advanced ethical hacking techniques, such as social engineering, advanced malware analysis, and exploitation of zero-day vulnerabilities, became essential skills for bug hunters. Additionally, the integration of artificial intelligence and machine learning in ethical hacking tools further enhanced the efficiency and accuracy of vulnerability detection.

1.2.9 Legal and Regulatory Recognition

Ethical hacking gained legal recognition in many jurisdictions, and laws protecting the rights of ethical hackers were introduced. Governments and organizations began embracing ethical hacking as a proactive measure to strengthen cybersecurity. Additionally, ethical hacking became a key component of compliance and risk management frameworks in various industries.

1.2.10 The Ongoing Evolution

The evolution of ethical hacking is ongoing, fueled by continuous advancements in technology and the ever-changing cyber threat landscape. Ethical hackers remain at the forefront of cybersecurity efforts, constantly adapting their skills and methodologies to stay ahead of emerging threats.

In conclusion, ethical hacking has come a long way from its early beginnings as a curiosity-driven exploration of technology to a structured and professional practice aimed at securing digital systems. The evolution of ethical hacking reflects the growing importance of cybersecurity in our digital age, and ethical hackers play a vital role in safeguarding the integrity of our interconnected world. As technology continues to advance, ethical hacking will continue to evolve, shaping the future of cybersecurity and providing critical defense against cyber threats.

1.3 Importance of Bug Bounty Programs

Bug bounty programs have emerged as a critical and impactful component of modern cybersecurity strategies. These programs offer a proactive and collaborative approach to identifying and addressing security vulnerabilities in digital systems. The importance of bug bounty programs can be understood through the following key aspects:

1.3.1 Detecting Vulnerabilities Proactively

Bug bounty programs empower organizations to detect vulnerabilities proactively. Instead of waiting for cyberattacks to occur, organizations invite ethical hackers to conduct controlled security assessments. This proactive approach enables the identification of potential security flaws before malicious actors can exploit them, reducing the risk of data breaches and cyber incidents.

1.3.2 Harnessing the Power of the Crowd

Bug bounty programs tap into the collective knowledge and expertise of the global cybersecurity community. By engaging ethical hackers from diverse backgrounds and skill sets, organizations benefit from a wide range of perspectives, increasing the likelihood of identifying complex and hard-to-detect vulnerabilities.

1.3.3 Cost-Effectiveness

Bug bounty programs offer a cost-effective alternative to traditional security assessments and penetration testing. Engaging a bug bounty community can be more efficient and economical than maintaining an in-house security team or hiring external consultants for periodic assessments. Bug bounties also eliminate the need for ongoing investments in expensive security infrastructure.

1.3.4 Encouraging Responsible Disclosure

Ethical hackers who participate in bug bounty programs commit to responsible disclosure. Instead of exploiting vulnerabilities for malicious purposes, they follow a structured process to report their findings to the organization hosting the program. This responsible disclosure approach gives organizations the opportunity to remediate vulnerabilities promptly, protecting user data and maintaining their reputation.

1.3.5 Continuous Improvement of Security

Bug bounty programs promote a culture of continuous improvement in cybersecurity. By running ongoing programs or engaging in periodic assessments, organizations constantly evaluate and enhance their security measures. This iterative process allows organizations to stay ahead of emerging threats and adapt to evolving cyber attack techniques.

1.3.6 Public Trust and Reputation

Having a bug bounty program demonstrates an organization's commitment to security and user trust. Publicly announcing the existence of a bug bounty program shows that the organization takes security seriously and is willing to invest in identifying and resolving vulnerabilities. This commitment enhances the organization's reputation among customers, partners, and stakeholders.

1.3.7 Identifying Zero-Day Vulnerabilities

Bug bounty programs are instrumental in identifying zero-day vulnerabilities, which are previously unknown and unpatched security flaws. By incentivizing ethical hackers to report such vulnerabilities, organizations can address them promptly and prevent potential large-scale attacks by malicious actors.

1.3.8 Wide Scope of Coverage

Bug bounty programs can cover a wide range of assets, including web applications, mobile apps, APIs, cloud infrastructure, IoT devices, and even physical security systems. This broad scope allows organizations to comprehensively assess their entire digital ecosystem, leaving no critical aspect unchecked.

1.3.9 Support for Compliance and Regulations

Bug bounty programs align with various compliance frameworks and regulatory requirements. Organizations in industries such as finance, healthcare, and government can demonstrate their commitment to security and compliance by engaging in bug bounty programs.

1.3.10 Fostering Collaboration and Community Building

Bug bounty programs foster collaboration and community building within the cybersecurity ecosystem. Ethical hackers, program owners, and bug bounty platform operators interact and exchange knowledge, contributing to a stronger and more cohesive cybersecurity community.

In conclusion, bug bounty programs play a crucial role in modern cybersecurity practices. They provide organizations with a proactive and cost-effective means to identify and address vulnerabilities, harness the collective expertise of the global cybersecurity community, and continuously improve their security measures. By encouraging responsible disclosure and fostering collaboration, bug bounty programs enhance the overall cybersecurity landscape and contribute to a safer digital environment for users worldwide.

1.4 Types of Bug Bounty Programs

Bug bounty programs come in various forms, tailored to the specific needs and goals of organizations. Each type of bug bounty program has its unique characteristics, scope, and rewards structure. Let's explore some of the most common types of bug bounty programs:

1.4.1 Public Bug Bounty Programs

Public bug bounty programs are open to the wider ethical hacking community. In these programs, any ethical hacker can participate, regardless of their background or affiliation. Public bug bounty programs are typically hosted by large technology companies, social media platforms, and organizations with a significant online presence. They offer monetary rewards, recognition, and sometimes bug bounty swag to ethical hackers who identify and responsibly disclose vulnerabilities.

1.4.2 Private Bug Bounty Programs

Private bug bounty programs are invitation-only programs that restrict participation to a select group of ethical hackers. These programs are commonly employed by organizations that prefer to work with a trusted and vetted community of researchers. Private bug bounty programs allow organizations to maintain tighter control over the scope of testing and establish deeper relationships with skilled bug hunters.

1.4.3 Time-Bound Bug Bounty Programs

Time-bound bug bounty programs have a specific duration during which ethical hackers can participate and submit their findings. These programs are often launched to address specific security concerns, such as the release of a new product, major software update, or hosting a special event. The limited timeframe motivates bug hunters to focus their efforts within the defined period, encouraging a surge of activity during the program's duration.

1.4.4 Continuous Bug Bounty Programs

Continuous bug bounty programs operate indefinitely, inviting ethical hackers to participate and submit vulnerability reports on an ongoing basis. These programs are particularly popular among organizations that prioritize continuous security assessment and want to maintain a consistent flow of vulnerability reports. Continuous programs enable bug hunters to engage with the organization's assets continuously, fostering long-term collaboration.

1.4.5 Triage-Only Bug Bounty Programs

Triage-only bug bounty programs focus on vulnerability submission triage, where ethical hackers primarily submit their findings for assessment and verification by a dedicated team of security analysts. While bug hunters may not receive direct financial rewards for triage submissions, they contribute to the overall security posture of the organization and may receive recognition for their valuable contributions.

1.4.6 Vulnerability Disclosure Programs (VDPs)

Vulnerability Disclosure Programs, also known as Responsible Disclosure Programs, are distinct from traditional bug bounty programs. Instead of offering monetary rewards, VDPs focus on providing a secure and responsible channel for the public to report security vulnerabilities. Organizations with VDPs commit to investigating and remedying vulnerabilities while offering ethical hackers the satisfaction of making a positive impact on cybersecurity.

1.4.7 Coordinated Vulnerability Disclosure (CVD) Programs

Coordinated Vulnerability Disclosure programs encourage open and transparent communication between the ethical hacker and the organization. Ethical hackers report their findings to the organization and agree to withhold public disclosure until the organization has had a reasonable opportunity to address the issue. CVD programs aim to foster cooperation and understanding between researchers and organizations, creating a safer environment for all parties involved.

1.4.8 Point-Based Bug Bounty Programs

Point-based bug bounty programs assign point values to different types of vulnerabilities based on their severity and impact. Ethical hackers accumulate points for each valid submission, and the rewards are calculated based on the total points earned. Point-based programs enable organizations to categorize vulnerabilities and allocate rewards accordingly, providing a structured and scalable approach to bug hunting.

1.4.9 Invitation-Only Challenges

Some bug bounty platforms host invitation-only challenges where top-performing ethical hackers are invited to participate in exclusive events or competitions. These challenges often offer substantial rewards and are used to engage elite bug hunters, promote healthy competition, and identify high-impact vulnerabilities in a competitive environment.

In conclusion, the types of bug bounty programs vary in scope, accessibility, and structure. Organizations can choose the most suitable type based on their goals, security requirements, and budget. Whether public or private, time-bound or continuous, bug bounty programs are essential components of a robust cybersecurity strategy, harnessing the collective expertise of ethical hackers to secure digital systems and protect user data.

Chapter 2: Preparing for Bug Bounty Hunting

In the exhilarating world of bug bounty hunting, success favors the prepared mind. Aspiring bug hunters must equip themselves with a diverse skill set, fortified by a strong foundation in cybersecurity and technical expertise. Welcome to Chapter 2 of "Bug Bounty Unleashed: Mastering the Art of Ethical Hacking and Rewards." Here, we delve into the essential steps required to prepare for a successful bug bounty hunting journey.

Building a Strong Cybersecurity Foundation

To embark on your bug bounty hunting adventure, a solid understanding of cybersecurity fundamentals is paramount. In this chapter, we will explore the principles of information security, cryptography, network protocols, and web application architecture. By mastering these foundational concepts, you will lay the groundwork for a rewarding and impactful bug hunting experience.

Mastering Programming Languages and Tools

A bug hunter's toolkit is incomplete without proficiency in programming languages and cybersecurity tools. In this section, we guide you through the essential languages like Python, JavaScript, and SQL, empowering you to wield them effectively in discovering and exploiting vulnerabilities. Additionally, we explore a plethora of cybersecurity tools that will become invaluable assets in your bug bounty hunting endeavors.

Creating a Secure Testing Environment

Safety first! In bug bounty hunting, a secure testing environment is essential to avoid unintended consequences and collateral damage. This chapter introduces you to various virtualization technologies and sandboxing solutions that allow you to create isolated testing environments for your ethical hacking exploits. Whether it's setting up virtual machines or configuring containers, you will be well-prepared to conduct your testing safely and responsibly.

Ethical Hacking Certifications and Training

To stand out as a skilled bug bounty hunter, obtaining relevant certifications and undergoing specialized training can significantly bolster your expertise and credibility. We explore renowned certifications such as Certified Ethical Hacker (CEH), Offensive Security Certified Professional (OSCP), and more, guiding you in choosing the certifications best suited for your bug bounty hunting goals. Moreover, we discuss valuable training resources and platforms to enhance your knowledge and stay ahead in the dynamic field of cybersecurity.

Challenging the Boundaries, Embracing the Opportunities

In this chapter's conclusion, we emphasize the importance of continuous learning and the pursuit of hands-on experiences. Aspiring bug bounty hunters must challenge their own boundaries and embrace opportunities to practice their skills in real-world scenarios. We encourage you to participate in capture-the-flag (CTF) competitions, hackathons, and bug bounty challenges to refine your skills and build the confidence necessary to thrive in the bug hunting landscape.

The journey to becoming a proficient bug bounty hunter begins with solid preparation. In Chapter 2, we equip you with the tools, knowledge, and mindset required to embark on your bug bounty hunting quest. Remember, preparation is the key that unlocks the door to success in the captivating realm of ethical hacking.

2.1 Building a Strong Cybersecurity Foundation

Establishing a robust cybersecurity foundation is crucial for organizations to defend against a growing array of cyber threats. A strong cybersecurity framework provides the groundwork for protecting sensitive data, ensuring business continuity, and safeguarding customer trust. Here are key elements to consider when building a strong cybersecurity foundation:

2.1.1 Risk Assessment and Threat Modeling

Begin by conducting a comprehensive risk assessment to identify potential vulnerabilities and threats specific to your organization. This involves evaluating the critical assets, data, and systems that require protection. Threat modeling can help simulate potential attack scenarios, enabling you to prioritize security efforts and allocate resources effectively.

2.1.2 Security Policies and Procedures

Develop clear and comprehensive cybersecurity policies and procedures that outline the guidelines for secure operations, user behavior, and data handling. These policies should cover aspects such as password management, data encryption, employee training, and incident response. Regularly update and communicate these policies to all relevant personnel to ensure everyone is aware of their responsibilities in maintaining security.

2.1.3 Employee Training and Awareness

Invest in ongoing cybersecurity training and awareness programs for all employees. Human error is a significant factor in security breaches, so educating staff about common threats, phishing attacks, and best practices can mitigate risks. Regularly remind employees of the importance of security protocols and the role they play in maintaining a secure environment.

2.1.4 Access Control and Authentication

Implement strong access control mechanisms to restrict user access to sensitive data and systems. Use multi-factor authentication (MFA) to add an extra layer of security, requiring users to provide multiple forms of identification before accessing critical resources. Regularly review user access privileges and remove unnecessary permissions to reduce the attack surface.

2.1.5 Network Security

Secure the organization's network infrastructure by implementing firewalls, intrusion detection/prevention systems, and regular network monitoring. Segment the network to limit the lateral movement of attackers in case of a breach. Encourage the use of virtual private networks (VPNs) for remote access, especially when accessing sensitive information.

2.1.6 Patch Management

Keep all software, applications, and operating systems up to date with the latest security patches. Regularly review and apply security updates to mitigate vulnerabilities that could be exploited by attackers. Automated patch management solutions can streamline this process and ensure timely updates.

2.1.7 Data Encryption

Utilize strong encryption methods to protect sensitive data, both at rest and in transit. Encrypt data stored in databases, on portable devices, and during communication between systems. Robust encryption practices ensure that even if data is compromised, it remains indecipherable to unauthorized individuals.

2.1.8 Incident Response Plan

Develop a well-defined incident response plan that outlines the steps to be taken in the event of a cybersecurity incident. The plan should include procedures for detecting, responding, and recovering from security breaches. Conduct periodic simulations and drills to test the effectiveness of the incident response plan and ensure staff is prepared to handle real-life incidents.

2.1.9 Regular Security Audits and Assessments

Perform regular security audits and assessments to evaluate the effectiveness of your cybersecurity measures. Engage third-party security experts or conduct internal assessments to identify weaknesses, gaps, and areas for improvement. Use the findings to refine and enhance your cybersecurity strategies continuously.

2.1.10 Collaborate with the Cybersecurity Community

Engage with the broader cybersecurity community, participate in bug bounty programs, and collaborate with ethical hackers to identify vulnerabilities in your systems. The collective knowledge of the cybersecurity community can provide valuable insights and help strengthen your cybersecurity defenses.

By implementing these fundamental elements, organizations can build a strong cybersecurity foundation that protects against evolving cyber threats, secures sensitive data, and ensures the continuity of business operations. Building a culture of security awareness and continuously improving security measures will enhance an organization's resilience in the face of the ever-changing cybersecurity landscape.

2.2 Mastering Programming Languages and Tools

In the realm of cybersecurity, mastering programming languages and tools is essential for cybersecurity professionals and ethical hackers. Proficiency in programming enables professionals to understand and analyze code, build security solutions, and identify vulnerabilities effectively. Here are key programming languages and tools that are vital for cybersecurity experts:

2.2.1 Python

Python is a versatile and widely used programming language in the cybersecurity domain. Its simplicity, readability, and extensive libraries make it an ideal choice for various cybersecurity tasks. Python is commonly used for scripting, network scanning, automation, web scraping, and building security tools. It also plays a crucial role in data analysis and machine learning applications used in cybersecurity.

2.2.2 C and C++

C and C++ are foundational programming languages in cybersecurity due to their efficiency and close-to-the-hardware capabilities. They are commonly used for low-level programming, system-level development, and creating security-focused applications and tools. Understanding C and C++ is essential for analyzing and identifying vulnerabilities in native code and developing secure software.

2.2.3 JavaScript

JavaScript is a crucial language for web application security. As the primary scripting language for web development, it is essential for understanding how web applications function and detecting client-side vulnerabilities. Ethical hackers often use JavaScript for browser-based attacks, cross-site scripting (XSS) testing, and assessing web application security.

2.2.4 SQL

Structured Query Language (SQL) is crucial for understanding and identifying database-related vulnerabilities. As a standard language for managing and querying relational databases, SQL is essential for detecting and preventing SQL injection vulnerabilities, a prevalent threat to web applications.

2.2.5 Bash Scripting

Bash scripting is valuable for automating repetitive tasks and performing various operations in the Linux/Unix environment. Cybersecurity professionals use Bash scripts for log analysis, system monitoring, and custom security scripts. Understanding Bash is essential for working with command-line interfaces and shell scripting.

2.2.6 PowerShell

PowerShell is Microsoft's powerful scripting language and automation framework used primarily on Windows systems. It is essential for managing and securing Windows environments and can be leveraged for tasks such as incident response, system administration, and malware analysis on Windows systems.

2.2.7 Wireshark

Wireshark is a widely used network protocol analyzer that enables cybersecurity professionals to capture and analyze network traffic. It helps identify suspicious network activities, potential security threats, and can assist in network forensics. Proficiency in Wireshark is valuable for analyzing packet-level data and understanding network vulnerabilities.

2.2.8 Metasploit

Metasploit is a well-known penetration testing framework that assists ethical hackers in discovering and exploiting vulnerabilities in systems. Mastering Metasploit allows professionals to simulate real-world cyberattacks and assess an organization's security posture effectively.

2.2.9 Nmap

Nmap is a popular open-source network scanning tool used for network discovery and security auditing. It enables cybersecurity professionals to identify open ports, potential vulnerabilities, and network topology, providing valuable information for securing networks.

2.2.10 Burp Suite

Burp Suite is a powerful web application security testing tool used to identify and assess web application vulnerabilities. It helps ethical hackers perform security assessments, including web application scanning, crawling, and identifying potential security flaws like SQL injection, XSS, and CSRF.

Mastering these programming languages and tools allows cybersecurity professionals to analyze, secure, and defend against cyber threats effectively. By combining programming expertise with a deep understanding of cybersecurity principles, professionals can create robust security solutions and enhance an organization's cybersecurity posture. Continuous learning and hands-on experience with these tools are key to staying ahead in the dynamic and evolving field of cybersecurity.

2.3 Creating a Secure Testing Environment

Creating a secure testing environment is crucial for cybersecurity professionals, ethical hackers, and organizations seeking to assess and improve their security measures effectively. A secure testing environment provides a controlled and isolated space to conduct security assessments, penetration testing, and vulnerability scanning without impacting production systems or exposing sensitive data. Here are essential steps to create a secure testing environment:

Isolation and Segmentation: Ensure that the testing environment is physically or logically isolated from the production network. Use separate network segments or virtual local area networks (VLANs) to prevent unauthorized access between the testing environment and the production environment.

Virtualization and Containerization: Embrace virtualization and containerization technologies to create isolated and reproducible testing environments. Tools like VMware, VirtualBox, or Docker allow you to run multiple virtual machines or containers on a single physical host, making it easier to manage and control the testing environment.

Hardware and Software Requirements: Ensure that the hardware and software used in the testing environment mirror the production environment as closely as possible. This ensures that security assessments are conducted in a realistic environment, capturing potential vulnerabilities that could exist in the real-world scenario.

Version Control: Use version control systems, such as Git, to manage the configuration and code changes in the testing environment. This helps maintain consistency, track changes, and revert to a known state if issues arise during testing.

Limited Internet Connectivity: Minimize internet connectivity in the testing environment to reduce the risk of malicious activities and unauthorized data transfers. If internet access is required for certain tests, consider using a separate and restricted internet connection.

Access Controls: Implement strict access controls in the testing environment. Limit access only to authorized personnel involved in security assessments. Use strong authentication mechanisms, like multi-factor authentication (MFA), to ensure that only authorized users can access the testing environment.

Data Sanitization: Before conducting tests, remove or sanitize any sensitive or personally identifiable information (PII) from the testing environment. Replace real data with dummy or fictional data to prevent potential data breaches or privacy violations during testing.

Backup and Recovery: Regularly back up the testing environment to ensure data integrity and facilitate quick recovery in case of any mishaps during testing. Test recovery procedures to ensure that the environment can be restored to a known state if needed.

Network Monitoring and Logging: Implement network monitoring and logging in the testing environment to capture any suspicious activities or potential security incidents. Analyzing logs can provide valuable insights into the effectiveness of security measures and help identify potential vulnerabilities.

Compliance with Legal and Ethical Standards: Ensure that the testing environment complies with all relevant legal, ethical, and regulatory standards. Obtain proper authorization from stakeholders and seek legal advice when necessary, especially when conducting assessments on third-party systems.

Periodic Security Assessments: Regularly assess the security of the testing environment itself to identify any vulnerabilities or misconfigurations. Treat the testing environment as a critical component of the overall security posture and apply security patches and updates as needed.

By following these steps, organizations and cybersecurity professionals can create a secure testing environment that facilitates comprehensive security assessments and helps identify and remediate vulnerabilities effectively. A secure testing environment is essential for improving an organization's cybersecurity defenses and ensuring a safe and resilient digital infrastructure.

2.4 Ethical Hacking Certifications and Training

Ethical hacking certifications and training are essential for individuals seeking to enter or advance in the field of cybersecurity and ethical hacking. These certifications validate the expertise, skills, and knowledge required to identify vulnerabilities, conduct security assessments, and responsibly disclose findings. Here are some of the most recognized ethical hacking certifications and the importance of training:

Certified Ethical Hacker (CEH): Offered by EC-Council, the CEH certification is one of the most widely recognized and sought-after certifications in ethical hacking. It covers various topics, including penetration testing, network security, web application security, and system hacking. CEH provides a comprehensive foundation in ethical hacking and is ideal for beginners.

CompTIA Security+: While not specifically an ethical hacking certification, CompTIA Security+ covers fundamental cybersecurity principles and practices, including ethical hacking techniques. It is an entry-level certification that establishes a solid understanding of cybersecurity concepts and prepares individuals for more advanced certifications.

Offensive Security Certified Professional (OSCP): Offered by Offensive Security, the OSCP certification is highly regarded in the industry and is considered one of the most challenging certifications to achieve. It involves a hands-on exam where candidates must exploit vulnerabilities in a controlled lab environment, demonstrating practical proficiency in ethical hacking.

Certified Information Systems Security Professional (CISSP): While not focused solely on ethical hacking, the CISSP certification is a globally recognized credential for information security professionals. It covers various security domains, including ethical hacking techniques, and is suitable for experienced professionals seeking a broader understanding of cybersecurity.

Certified Penetration Tester (CPT): Offered by the Information Assurance Certification Review Board (IACRB), the CPT certification focuses specifically on penetration testing skills and methodologies. It is designed for individuals who wish to specialize in ethical hacking and penetration testing.

GIAC Penetration Tester (GPEN): Offered by the Global Information Assurance Certification (GIAC), the GPEN certification validates skills in conducting ethical hacking and penetration tests. It emphasizes real-world application and hands-on practical knowledge.

eLearnSecurity Certified Professional Penetration Tester (eCPPT): The eCPPT certification, offered by eLearnSecurity, is a practical and hands-on certification that covers penetration testing methodologies, techniques, and tools. It is suitable for individuals looking for practical experience in penetration testing.

The importance of training in ethical hacking cannot be overstated. While certifications demonstrate theoretical knowledge, hands-on training equips individuals with practical skills needed to identify and exploit vulnerabilities. Many certification programs offer hands-on labs and practical exercises, allowing candidates to gain real-world experience in a controlled environment.

Continuous learning and keeping up-to-date with the latest cybersecurity trends and threats are also crucial. Ethical hackers should consider attending workshops, conferences, and online courses to stay current with emerging techniques and best practices.

In conclusion, ethical hacking certifications and training provide professionals with the knowledge and skills necessary to excel in the field of cybersecurity. These credentials not only validate expertise but also demonstrate a commitment to ethical practices and responsible hacking. Combined with hands-on training and continuous learning, individuals can build successful careers as ethical hackers, contributing to the ever-growing need for cybersecurity expertise in today's digital landscape.

Chapter 3: Ethical Hacking Methodology

In the world of ethical hacking, success is not merely the result of chance or luck; it is a meticulously planned and systematic endeavor. Welcome to Chapter 3 of "Bug Bounty Unleashed: Mastering the Art of Ethical Hacking and Rewards." Here, we embark on a journey into the heart of ethical hacking methodology—the structured approach followed by skilled bug bounty hunters to uncover vulnerabilities responsibly.

Understanding the Hacker Mindset and Approach

In this section, we dive into the mindset of ethical hackers, exploring how they think and approach challenges from a different perspective. By understanding the "hacker mindset," you will learn to think like the adversary, enabling you to anticipate potential weaknesses and vulnerabilities within a target system. Moreover, we will discuss the importance of creativity, persistence, and resourcefulness in the quest for uncovering critical bugs.

Footprinting and Information Gathering Techniques

Every successful ethical hacking expedition begins with meticulous information gathering. We will guide you through the process of footprinting, where you gather valuable intelligence about your target. From open-source intelligence (OSINT) to passive reconnaissance and active scanning, you will learn essential techniques to lay the groundwork for a successful bug hunting operation.

Scanning and Enumeration for Vulnerabilities

With reconnaissance complete, it's time to scan and enumerate the target for potential vulnerabilities. In this segment, we explore the tools and techniques that help identify open ports, services, and other potential entry points into the target system. You will understand the significance of detailed enumeration in uncovering security flaws and areas vulnerable to exploitation.

Exploitation and Post-Exploitation Phases

This is the phase where the rubber meets the road—the exploitation and post-exploitation phases. We delve into the art of exploiting discovered vulnerabilities responsibly, ensuring that you do not cause harm while demonstrating the severity of the bug to program owners. Furthermore, we explore the post-exploitation techniques that ethical hackers employ to maintain access, escalate privileges, and gather evidence for comprehensive bug reports.

The Importance of Methodical Documentation

Throughout this chapter, we emphasize the significance of methodical documentation. Accurate and comprehensive documentation is the backbone of effective bug hunting. We guide you on how to keep meticulous records of your findings, the steps you took, and the outcomes you encountered during the ethical hacking process. These detailed records will prove indispensable when reporting your discoveries to program owners.

Balancing Risk and Responsibility

Ethical hacking is a dual responsibility—to identify vulnerabilities while ensuring no harm is done in the process. In this section, we explore the ethical considerations and risks associated with hacking activities. By striking a delicate balance between risk and responsibility, you will conduct your bug bounty hunting ventures with integrity and professionalism.

In this chapter's conclusion, you will be equipped with a solid ethical hacking methodology—a structured approach that ethical hackers follow to navigate the complexities of bug hunting. By adopting this methodical mindset, you will be well-prepared to uncover vulnerabilities responsibly, secure digital systems, and reap the rewards that await skilled bug bounty hunters.

3.1 The Hacker Mindset and Approach

The term "hacker" has evolved over the years and carries different connotations. In the context of cybersecurity and ethical hacking, a hacker refers to someone with a unique mindset and approach to problem-solving. Understanding the hacker mindset is essential for ethical hackers as it allows them to think like adversaries, identify potential vulnerabilities, and adopt a proactive security stance. Here are key aspects of the hacker mindset and approach:

Curiosity and Inquisitiveness: Hackers possess an innate curiosity and a desire to understand how things work. They constantly question systems, applications, and networks to explore potential weaknesses and discover unconventional paths to achieve their goals.

Problem-Solving Skills: Hackers are natural problem solvers. They enjoy challenges and view security as a puzzle to be solved. They approach cybersecurity with a creative and innovative mindset, seeking unique and unexpected solutions.

Persistence and Determination: The hacker mindset involves persistence and determination in the face of obstacles. Ethical hackers don't give up easily;

they keep trying different approaches until they achieve their objectives, whether it's identifying a vulnerability or crafting an exploit.

Reverse Engineering: Hackers are skilled at reverse engineering, which involves analyzing systems and software to understand their inner workings. This allows them to identify weaknesses and potential attack vectors that might not be immediately apparent.

Continuous Learning: The cybersecurity landscape is constantly evolving, and hackers are aware of the importance of staying up-to-date with the latest technologies and attack techniques. They continuously learn and adapt their skills to keep pace with emerging threats.

Ethical Approach: Ethical hackers understand the responsibility that comes with their skills and knowledge. They adhere to a strict code of ethics and engage in responsible disclosure of vulnerabilities, ensuring that their actions do not cause harm.

Outside-the-Box Thinking: Hackers think outside the box and are willing to explore unconventional methods to achieve their objectives. They understand that attackers don't always follow the rules, and to defend against them effectively, they must anticipate unexpected tactics.

No Assumptions: Hackers approach cybersecurity with an open mind and avoid making assumptions about system security. They test thoroughly and validate their findings before drawing conclusions.

Understanding the Adversary: Effective hackers put themselves in the shoes of potential adversaries. They think like malicious actors, anticipating their motivations, techniques, and targets. This "red team" perspective helps ethical hackers identify weak points and areas of vulnerability.

Meticulousness and Attention to Detail: Hackers pay close attention to detail. They carefully analyze system behavior, code, and network traffic, leaving no stone unturned in their pursuit of identifying and exploiting vulnerabilities.

Continuous Testing and Improvement: The hacker approach involves continuous testing and improvement. Ethical hackers understand that security is an ongoing process, and they strive to identify and address vulnerabilities before attackers do.

The hacker mindset, when channeled ethically and responsibly, is a powerful asset in the field of cybersecurity. Ethical hackers use their unique perspective and approach to proactively identify and mitigate security risks, helping organizations protect their digital assets and stay one step ahead of potential threats. By adopting the hacker mindset, ethical hackers contribute positively to a safer and more secure digital environment for everyone.

3.2 Footprinting and Information Gathering Techniques

Footprinting is the process of gathering information about a target system, network, or organization with the intention of understanding its structure, vulnerabilities, and potential attack surfaces. Ethical hackers use footprinting techniques to assess an organization's online presence and identify potential entry points for further assessment. Here are some common footprinting and information gathering techniques:

Open-Source Intelligence (OSINT): OSINT involves gathering information from publicly available sources, such as search engines, social media, online forums, and public records. Ethical hackers use OSINT to obtain details about the target organization, including employee names, contact information, email addresses, and network configurations.

DNS Footprinting: Domain Name System (DNS) footprinting involves querying DNS servers to obtain information about a target's domain names, subdomains, and associated IP addresses. Tools like nslookup and dig are commonly used for DNS footprinting.

Whois Lookup: A Whois lookup provides registration details of domain names, including the owner's contact information, registration date, and DNS servers. Ethical hackers use Whois lookups to gather information about the target organization's domain names.

Website Analysis: Analyzing the target organization's website can reveal valuable information, such as the technologies used, subdomains, employee details, and potentially vulnerable web applications. Tools like BuiltWith and Wappalyzer aid in website analysis.

Social Engineering: Social engineering techniques involve manipulating individuals to divulge sensitive information or access credentials. Ethical hackers use controlled social engineering engagements to assess an organization's susceptibility to such attacks.

Network Scanning: Network scanning involves identifying active hosts, open ports, and services on the target network. Port scanning tools like Nmap help ethical hackers gather valuable information about the target's network infrastructure.

Google Hacking (Google Dorking): Google Hacking involves using specific search queries (Google dorks) to find sensitive information, misconfigurations, and vulnerable systems indexed by search engines. Google Hacking Database (GHDB) contains a collection of common dorks.

Email Footprinting: Email footprinting involves identifying email addresses associated with the target organization. This information can be used for social engineering, phishing, and identifying potential targets for further assessment.

Traceroute: Traceroute traces the path that packets take from the attacker's system to the target system, revealing the network topology and potential points of entry.

Archive and Pastebin Searches: Searching internet archives and Pastebin can uncover sensitive information or leaked credentials related to the target organization.

Shodan and Censys Searches: Shodan and Censys are search engines that allow ethical hackers to find devices connected to the internet, such as servers, webcams, and IoT devices. This helps identify potential entry points for further assessment.

It is essential to note that ethical hackers must adhere to a strict code of ethics and legal guidelines when conducting footprinting and information gathering. Unauthorized access to sensitive information or systems is illegal and unethical. Ethical hackers should seek proper authorization from the target organization and conduct their assessments within the scope defined by the organization.

Footprinting and information gathering are the initial stages of the ethical hacking process, providing valuable insights for subsequent stages of assessment and vulnerability identification. By employing these techniques responsibly and ethically, ethical hackers play a crucial role in helping organizations strengthen their cybersecurity defenses.

3.3 Scanning and Enumeration for Vulnerabilities

Scanning and enumeration are critical phases in the ethical hacking process, where cybersecurity professionals actively search for vulnerabilities and weaknesses in the target system or network. These phases involve systematic and controlled techniques to identify potential entry points for exploitation. Let's explore scanning and enumeration for vulnerabilities:

1. Network Scanning:

- **Port Scanning**: Ethical hackers use tools like Nmap to scan for open ports on target systems. Open ports may indicate services running on the system, and each open port represents a potential attack surface.

- **Vulnerability Scanning**: Vulnerability scanning tools, such as Nessus or OpenVAS, identify known vulnerabilities in the target system by comparing its configuration and software against a database of known security issues.

2. Enumeration:

- **User Enumeration**: In this phase, ethical hackers attempt to identify valid usernames on target systems. Tools like enum4linux can extract user account information from Windows systems.
- **Network Enumeration**: Ethical hackers gather information about network resources, shares, and services available on the target network. Tools like Enum4linux and SMBclient are useful for gathering such information from Windows systems.
- **Service Enumeration**: During service enumeration, ethical hackers attempt to gain detailed information about the services running on open ports. This includes version information and configuration details that may reveal potential vulnerabilities.
- **DNS Enumeration**: DNS enumeration involves querying DNS servers to gather information about the target's domain names, subdomains,

and associated IP addresses. Tools like DNSenum aid in DNS enumeration.

- **SNMP Enumeration**: Simple Network Management Protocol (SNMP) enumeration involves querying SNMP-enabled devices to gather information about the target's network devices, including routers, switches, and servers.

3. Banner Grabbing:

Banner grabbing is the process of capturing service banners or headers from open ports. The information obtained may include software versions and configurations that can be useful for identifying known vulnerabilities.

4. Web Application Scanning:

Ethical hackers use web vulnerability scanners, such as OWASP ZAP and Burp Suite, to automatically identify common web application vulnerabilities, such as SQL injection, cross-site scripting (XSS), and insecure configurations.

5. Wireless Network Scanning:

For wireless networks, ethical hackers use tools like Aircrack-ng or Kismet to scan for available wireless access points and identify potential security weaknesses in their configurations.

6. Enumeration of File Shares:

Ethical hackers attempt to enumerate shared resources on the target network. Tools like SMBclient and enum4linux can help identify shared directories and files.

7. LDAP Enumeration:

For organizations using Lightweight Directory Access Protocol (LDAP), ethical hackers may use tools like ldapsearch to query the LDAP directory and obtain information about users and groups.

It is important to emphasize that scanning and enumeration should always be conducted within the scope of the authorized engagement. Ethical hackers should obtain proper authorization from the target organization and strictly adhere to legal and ethical guidelines during the entire process. Unauthorized scanning and enumeration are not only illegal but can also disrupt target systems and networks, leading to unintended consequences. Responsible and ethical conduct in scanning and enumeration helps ensure a positive impact on cybersecurity and the overall safety of digital systems.

3.4 Exploitation and Post-Exploitation Phases

The exploitation and post-exploitation phases are critical components of ethical hacking, where cybersecurity professionals or ethical hackers attempt to gain unauthorized access to target systems to assess their security posture and demonstrate potential risks. These phases involve the controlled use of vulnerabilities to penetrate systems and gather valuable information. It is essential to note that these activities should only be conducted with proper authorization from the target organization and should strictly adhere to ethical and legal guidelines.

1. Exploitation Phase:

- **Exploiting Vulnerabilities**: In this phase, ethical hackers use known vulnerabilities discovered during the scanning and enumeration phase to gain unauthorized access to target systems. Exploits can take various forms, such as buffer overflows, SQL injection, remote code execution, or privilege escalation exploits.
- **Payload Delivery**: Once a vulnerability is identified, ethical hackers deliver a payload, such as a malicious code or script, to exploit the vulnerability and gain control over the target system.

- **Metasploit Framework**: The Metasploit Framework is a widely used tool for developing, testing, and executing exploits. It helps ethical hackers automate and streamline the exploitation process.

2. Post-Exploitation Phase:

- **Maintaining Access**: After successful exploitation, ethical hackers aim to maintain access to the compromised system for as long as possible. They use techniques to establish persistence, such as installing backdoors or creating additional user accounts.
- **Privilege Escalation**: Ethical hackers attempt to elevate their privileges on the compromised system to gain access to more sensitive data and resources. This involves exploiting vulnerabilities that allow the attacker to escalate their privileges from a low-level user to an administrator or root user.
- **Lateral Movement**: In some cases, ethical hackers may explore other systems on the network from the compromised system, seeking opportunities to move laterally and gain access to more valuable targets.
- **Data Exfiltration**: Ethical hackers may attempt to exfiltrate sensitive data from the compromised system or network to demonstrate the potential impact of a security breach.

3. Maintaining Stealth:

Throughout the post-exploitation phase, ethical hackers strive to maintain a low profile and avoid detection by security monitoring systems and administrators. They may use anti-forensic techniques and other evasion methods to evade detection.

4. Documentation and Reporting:

Ethical hackers document each step of the exploitation and post-exploitation process, including the vulnerabilities exploited, the actions taken, and the data accessed. Comprehensive reporting is essential to provide the target organization with detailed information about the security weaknesses identified and recommendations for remediation.

5. Ethical and Responsible Conduct:

Throughout the entire exploitation and post-exploitation phases, ethical hackers must maintain ethical and responsible conduct. They should avoid causing harm, damaging systems, or disrupting critical services during their assessments. The primary objective is to help the target organization improve its security posture and protect against real-world threats.

It is crucial to emphasize that the exploitation and post-exploitation phases should only be performed with explicit authorization and in a controlled environment. Unauthorized exploitation of vulnerabilities or unauthorized access to systems is illegal and unethical. Ethical hacking engagements must follow the scope defined by the target organization and abide by all legal and ethical guidelines. Responsible conduct in these phases helps ensure a positive impact on cybersecurity while avoiding any negative consequences for the target organization.

Chapter 4: Types of Vulnerabilities and Exploits

In the ever-evolving landscape of cybersecurity, understanding the diverse array of vulnerabilities and exploits is the key to becoming a proficient bug bounty hunter. Welcome to Chapter 4 of "Bug Bounty Unleashed: Mastering the Art of Ethical Hacking and Rewards." In this chapter, we delve into the world of vulnerabilities—common weaknesses found in digital systems—and explore the methods employed by ethical hackers to exploit them responsibly.

Understanding Web Application Vulnerabilities

Web applications are the lifeblood of the digital world, but they also harbor various security weaknesses. In this section, we examine the most prevalent web application vulnerabilities, such as SQL injection, Cross-Site Scripting (XSS), Cross-Site Request Forgery (CSRF), and more. By understanding these vulnerabilities and the potential risks they pose, you will be well-equipped to safeguard web applications from malicious intrusions.

Exploiting Network Vulnerabilities

Networks form the backbone of modern communication, and their security is paramount. We explore network vulnerabilities, including misconfigurations, weak authentication mechanisms, and open ports, that can lead to unauthorized access. By gaining insights into network vulnerabilities and their exploitation techniques, you will be ready to fortify network infrastructures and protect sensitive data.

Probing Mobile Application Weaknesses

With the proliferation of mobile devices, securing mobile applications has become critical. In this segment, we focus on vulnerabilities specific to mobile apps, such as insecure data storage, insecure communication, and reverse engineering threats. As you explore the unique challenges of mobile application security, you will acquire the skills to enhance the resilience of mobile apps against potential attacks.

Hidden Dangers in IoT Devices and OT Systems

The Internet of Things (IoT) and Operational Technology (OT) have expanded the attack surface significantly, making them attractive targets for malicious hackers. We delve into the vulnerabilities inherent in IoT devices and OT systems, including weak authentication, firmware vulnerabilities, and lack of security updates. By addressing the challenges posed by these technologies, you will learn to safeguard the interconnected world of IoT and OT.

The Art of Responsible Exploitation

Ethical hackers must wield their knowledge responsibly, ensuring that they cause no harm while demonstrating the impact of discovered vulnerabilities. Throughout this chapter, we emphasize the importance of responsible exploitation—the controlled demonstration of vulnerabilities in a safe and ethical manner. By mastering responsible exploitation, you will be able to communicate the severity of bugs effectively without causing damage to the target system.

Becoming the Defender

As we conclude this chapter, we encourage you to view vulnerabilities through the lens of a defender. Understanding how adversaries exploit weaknesses will empower you to proactively secure systems and stay one step ahead in the relentless battle against cyber threats. By becoming both the hunter and the defender, you will transform into a formidable force in the bug bounty hunting landscape.

In this chapter, you have explored a myriad of vulnerabilities and the art of ethical exploitation. Armed with this knowledge, you will now be able to identify, assess, and responsibly exploit vulnerabilities, playing a vital role in securing the digital world one bug at a time.

4.1 Understanding Web Application Vulnerabilities

Understanding web application vulnerabilities is crucial for ethical hackers and cybersecurity professionals. Web applications are a primary target for attackers due to their widespread use and potential exposure of sensitive data. Identifying and mitigating these vulnerabilities is essential to ensure the security of web applications. Here are some common web application vulnerabilities:

1. Cross-Site Scripting (XSS):

XSS vulnerabilities allow attackers to inject malicious scripts into web pages viewed by other users. This can lead to unauthorized access, session hijacking, and data theft. XSS can be reflected or stored, depending on how the input is processed and displayed.

2. SQL Injection (SQLi):

SQL injection occurs when an attacker manipulates input fields to execute malicious SQL queries against the web application's database. Successful SQL injection can lead to unauthorized data access, modification, or deletion.

3. Cross-Site Request Forgery (CSRF):

CSRF vulnerabilities allow attackers to trick authenticated users into unknowingly sending forged HTTP requests to a web application. This can result in unauthorized actions performed on behalf of the victim user.

4. Insecure Direct Object References (IDOR):

IDOR vulnerabilities occur when an attacker can access and manipulate internal objects or resources directly, bypassing authorization controls. This can lead to unauthorized access to sensitive data or functionalities.

5. Security Misconfigurations:

Security misconfigurations arise when web applications are not properly configured, leaving them vulnerable to attacks. Examples include default credentials, directory listing, and unnecessary services exposed to the internet.

6. Server-Side Request Forgery (SSRF):

SSRF vulnerabilities enable attackers to make requests from the server to internal or external resources. This can lead to unauthorized access to internal systems or exfiltration of sensitive data.

7. Remote Code Execution (RCE):

RCE vulnerabilities allow attackers to execute arbitrary code on the server hosting the web application. This can result in complete control over the system and potential compromise of the entire server.

8. File Inclusion Vulnerabilities:

File inclusion vulnerabilities occur when an attacker can include files from the server's file system, leading to arbitrary code execution or unauthorized access to sensitive files.

9. Authentication and Session Management Issues:

Weak authentication mechanisms, session management flaws, or session fixation vulnerabilities can lead to unauthorized access to user accounts and sensitive data.

10. XML External Entity (XXE) Injection:

XXE vulnerabilities enable attackers to read sensitive files, perform SSRF attacks, or cause denial of service by exploiting XML parsing issues.

11. Insecure Deserialization:

Insecure deserialization vulnerabilities allow attackers to manipulate serialized data to execute arbitrary code or perform other malicious actions.

Understanding these web application vulnerabilities helps ethical hackers identify potential weaknesses and recommend appropriate security measures to mitigate them. Web application security testing, code reviews, and secure development practices are essential to ensuring robust and secure web applications. Regular security assessments and proactive measures are crucial to staying ahead of potential attackers and protecting sensitive data and user information.

4.2 Exploiting Network Vulnerabilities

Exploiting network vulnerabilities is a critical aspect of ethical hacking and cybersecurity assessments. Identifying and understanding these vulnerabilities helps ethical hackers assess the security posture of a network and helps organizations strengthen their defenses. Here are some common network vulnerabilities that ethical hackers may exploit:

1. Unpatched Software:

Exploiting vulnerabilities in unpatched software is a common attack vector. Ethical hackers identify systems running outdated software with known vulnerabilities and exploit them to gain unauthorized access.

2. Default Credentials:

Many devices and systems come with default usernames and passwords, which are often left unchanged by users. Ethical hackers attempt to gain access by using default credentials.

3. Weak Passwords:

Weak passwords are a significant security risk. Ethical hackers use various techniques like brute-force attacks and password cracking to guess or obtain weak passwords and gain unauthorized access.

4. Misconfigured Firewall Rules:

Misconfigured firewall rules can lead to unintended exposure of services to the internet or internal network. Ethical hackers identify and exploit such misconfigurations to bypass firewalls and access restricted resources.

5. Man-in-the-Middle (MitM) Attacks:

MitM attacks involve intercepting and altering communication between two parties. Ethical hackers may exploit weak encryption, unsecured Wi-Fi networks, or rogue access points to conduct MitM attacks.

6. ARP Spoofing/Poisoning:

ARP spoofing or poisoning involves manipulating the Address Resolution Protocol (ARP) cache to redirect network traffic. Ethical hackers use this technique to intercept and eavesdrop on network communications.

7. VLAN Hopping:

VLAN hopping exploits misconfigurations in switch configurations to gain unauthorized access to traffic from other VLANs.

8. SNMP Vulnerabilities:

Simple Network Management Protocol (SNMP) misconfigurations or weak community strings can provide unauthorized access to network devices.

9. DNS Vulnerabilities:

DNS vulnerabilities, such as cache poisoning or DNS hijacking, can be exploited by ethical hackers to redirect traffic or perform phishing attacks.

10. Buffer Overflows:

Buffer overflow vulnerabilities in network services can be exploited by ethical hackers to execute arbitrary code or crash systems.

11. Zero-Day Vulnerabilities:

Ethical hackers may encounter zero-day vulnerabilities, which are unknown to the vendor and lack patches. If discovered, they must handle them responsibly and disclose them to the vendor.

It is crucial to emphasize that ethical hackers should only exploit vulnerabilities within the scope defined by the target organization and with proper authorization. Unauthorized exploitation of network vulnerabilities is illegal and unethical. Ethical hacking engagements must follow the principles of responsible and ethical conduct to ensure the safety and security of the target organization's network and data. Ethical hackers play a crucial role in helping organizations identify and remediate network vulnerabilities, thus strengthening their cybersecurity defenses.

4.3 Probing Mobile Application Weaknesses

Probing mobile application weaknesses is an essential part of mobile application security testing. Mobile applications are prevalent, and they often handle sensitive user data, making them a prime target for attackers. Ethical hackers perform security assessments to identify and address vulnerabilities in mobile applications. Here are some common techniques for probing mobile application weaknesses:

1. Static Application Analysis:

Ethical hackers analyze the mobile application's binary code or source code without executing it. This involves scrutinizing the code for potential vulnerabilities, insecure coding practices, and sensitive information exposure.

2. Dynamic Application Analysis:

In dynamic analysis, ethical hackers run the mobile application on test devices or emulators. They monitor the application's behavior during runtime, including network requests, data storage, and interactions with external services. This helps identify potential security issues, such as insecure data transmission or excessive permissions.

3. Reverse Engineering:

Ethical hackers may reverse engineer the mobile application's binary code to understand its inner workings and identify potential vulnerabilities. Reverse engineering helps uncover hidden functionalities, encryption mechanisms, and potential security flaws.

4. Input Validation Testing:

Ethical hackers perform extensive input validation testing to identify vulnerabilities like injection attacks (SQL injection, XPath injection, etc.), buffer overflows, and data manipulation vulnerabilities.

5. Authentication and Authorization Testing:

Ethical hackers test the application's authentication and authorization mechanisms. They attempt to bypass authentication controls, brute-force passwords, and exploit flaws in session management.

6. Data Storage Analysis:

Ethical hackers examine how sensitive data is stored on the device or transmitted to backend servers. They look for issues like insecure data storage, clear-text passwords, and improper handling of cryptographic keys.

7. Network Traffic Analysis:

Ethical hackers intercept and analyze network traffic generated by the mobile application. This helps identify potential security weaknesses, unencrypted data transmission, and unauthorized data leakage.

8. Secure Communication Assessment:

Ethical hackers assess the implementation of secure communication protocols (e.g., SSL/TLS) within the mobile application to prevent eavesdropping and man-in-the-middle attacks.

9. Third-Party Library Assessment:

Many mobile applications rely on third-party libraries. Ethical hackers scrutinize these libraries for known vulnerabilities and weaknesses.

10. Platform-Specific Vulnerabilities:

Ethical hackers consider platform-specific vulnerabilities (iOS and Android) that could affect the security of the mobile application. For instance, they may investigate issues like jailbreaking/rooting, privilege escalation, and sandbox escape.

11. Business Logic Testing:

Ethical hackers assess the mobile application's business logic to identify vulnerabilities like transaction manipulation, account enumeration, and access control issues.

12. Compliance and Privacy Review:

Ethical hackers ensure that the mobile application complies with relevant privacy regulations and guidelines. They check for issues related to data privacy, consent management, and data retention.

It is essential to conduct mobile application security testing in a controlled environment with proper authorization from the mobile application's owner. Unauthorized probing of mobile application weaknesses is illegal and unethical. Ethical hackers play a crucial role in helping developers and organizations identify and remediate vulnerabilities, thus enhancing the security of mobile applications and protecting user data.

4.4 Hidden Dangers in IoT Devices and OT Systems

Hidden dangers in IoT (Internet of Things) devices and OT (Operational Technology) systems pose significant cybersecurity risks. As IoT devices and OT systems continue to proliferate across industries, they bring convenience and efficiency but also introduce new attack surfaces that malicious actors can exploit. Ethical hackers play a crucial role in identifying and addressing these hidden dangers to protect critical infrastructure and data. Here are some of the common hidden dangers in IoT devices and OT systems:

1. Weak Authentication and Authorization:

Many IoT devices and OT systems lack robust authentication and authorization mechanisms, making them vulnerable to unauthorized access and control. Weak default credentials and hardcoded passwords are common issues.

2. Lack of Security Updates and Patches:

Manufacturers often neglect providing regular security updates and patches for IoT devices and OT systems. This leaves these devices susceptible to known vulnerabilities that can be easily exploited.

3. Insecure Communication Protocols:

Inadequate or insecure communication protocols can expose sensitive data transmitted between IoT devices and backend systems. Lack of encryption may lead to data interception and manipulation.

4. Vulnerabilities in Third-Party Components:

IoT devices and OT systems frequently rely on third-party components and libraries, some of which may have known vulnerabilities. If left unaddressed, these vulnerabilities can be exploited to compromise the entire system.

5. Lack of Device Management and Monitoring:

Many IoT devices and OT systems lack proper device management and monitoring capabilities, making it challenging to detect and respond to security incidents promptly.

6. Physical Security Risks:

Physical access to IoT devices or OT systems can lead to potential tampering or unauthorized control, which may have severe consequences in critical infrastructures.

7. Insider Threats:

Insiders with access to IoT devices and OT systems may pose a significant threat. Malicious employees or contractors can intentionally exploit vulnerabilities or compromise security controls.

8. Lack of Security by Design:

Insecure design practices during the development of IoT devices and OT systems may result in weak security foundations that are difficult to address later.

9. Supply Chain Risks:

The complex supply chain involved in manufacturing and deploying IoT devices can introduce vulnerabilities and hidden dangers. Malicious actors may compromise components during the manufacturing process or distribution.

10. Lack of Security Awareness:

Users of IoT devices and operators of OT systems may not be aware of potential security risks and best practices, leading to unintentional security breaches.

11. Convergence of IT and OT:

The convergence of IT and OT systems blurs the lines between traditionally isolated networks, potentially exposing critical infrastructure to IT-related threats.

Addressing these hidden dangers requires a proactive and comprehensive approach to cybersecurity. Ethical hackers can play a vital role in identifying vulnerabilities and weaknesses in IoT devices and OT systems, enabling organizations to implement effective security measures. Regular security assessments, threat modeling, security training, and collaboration with manufacturers are essential to ensure the security and resilience of IoT devices and OT systems in today's interconnected world.

Chapter 5: Bug Bounty Platforms and Strategies

In the vast landscape of bug bounty hunting, navigating the diverse array of bug bounty platforms and crafting effective strategies is essential for success. Welcome to Chapter 5 of "Bug Bounty Unleashed: Mastering the Art of Ethical Hacking and Rewards." In this chapter, we explore the world of bug bounty platforms and equip you with the strategies to optimize your bug hunting endeavors.

Navigating Bug Bounty Platforms

Bug bounty platforms serve as the central hub for bug hunters and program owners to collaborate in a secure and controlled environment. We will guide you through popular bug bounty platforms, such as HackerOne, Bugcrowd, and Synack, examining their unique features, program structures, and reputation systems. By understanding the nuances of these platforms, you will be able to select those that align best with your bug hunting goals.

Target Selection and Scope Analysis

Effective bug hunting begins with strategic target selection and scope analysis. In this section, we discuss the significance of identifying suitable programs and understanding their specific scope and limitations. By honing your ability to analyze program guidelines, you will optimize your efforts, focusing on areas most likely to yield valuable vulnerabilities.

Bug Bounty Hunting Methodologies

Every successful bug hunter employs a distinct methodology to maximize their chances of success. We introduce you to various bug hunting methodologies, such as OWASP's Bug Bounty Hunting Methodology and the Recon-Exploit-Report (RER) approach. By adopting these proven strategies, you will streamline your bug hunting efforts and achieve more fruitful results.

Maximizing Efficiency with Automation Tools

As bug bounty hunting continues to evolve, automation tools have become indispensable assets for efficient bug hunters. We explore a range of automation tools and scripts, from vulnerability scanners to reconnaissance utilities, that can augment your bug hunting capabilities. By leveraging automation, you will boost your efficiency and uncover hidden vulnerabilities with greater speed and precision.

Challenging the Boundaries of Creativity

While methodologies and tools are crucial, creative thinking remains the heart of successful bug bounty hunting. In this segment, we encourage you to think outside the box, challenge assumptions, and explore unconventional avenues to uncover elusive vulnerabilities. Embracing creativity allows you to transcend boundaries and discover innovative ways to secure digital systems.

Building a Reputation in the Bug Bounty Community

In the interconnected world of bug bounty hunting, reputation holds significant value. We discuss the importance of building a positive reputation within the bug bounty community through professionalism, collaboration, and responsible disclosure. By fostering relationships with fellow hackers and program owners, you will gain recognition for your expertise and contributions.

Securing the Bounty: Negotiation and Reward Optimization

As you uncover vulnerabilities, securing the bounty becomes the next vital step. We guide you through effective negotiation strategies, ensuring you receive fair compensation for your discoveries. Moreover, we explore ways to optimize your rewards, whether through additional bonuses, acknowledgments, or even swag.

In this chapter's conclusion, you have delved into the intricacies of bug bounty platforms and honed your strategic bug hunting capabilities. Armed with a comprehensive understanding of these platforms and the strategies to navigate them effectively, you are now prepared to embark on bug hunting endeavors that transcend boundaries and reap the rewards that await skilled hunters.

5.1 Navigating Bug Bounty Platforms

Navigating bug bounty platforms is an essential skill for individuals participating in bug bounty programs. Bug bounty platforms serve as intermediaries between organizations seeking security assessments and ethical hackers who want to find and report vulnerabilities for monetary rewards. Understanding how these platforms work and how to navigate them effectively can significantly increase your chances of success as a bug bounty hunter. Here are some key points to consider when navigating bug bounty platforms:

1. Platform Selection:

There are several bug bounty platforms available, each with its unique features and clientele. Research and choose platforms that align with your expertise, interests, and target industries.

2. Program Scope and Rules:

Read and understand the bug bounty program's scope, rules, and guidelines. Focus on programs where you have expertise and ensure you comply with the rules to avoid disqualification.

3. Vulnerability Disclosure Policies:

Familiarize yourself with the platform's vulnerability disclosure policies and guidelines. Understand how to responsibly disclose vulnerabilities and the timeframes for reporting.

4. Reputation and Ranking:

Bug bounty platforms often have ranking systems based on the number and severity of reported vulnerabilities. Building a positive reputation and achieving higher rankings can increase your visibility to organizations and boost your earning potential.

5. Bug Types and Rewards:

Different platforms offer rewards for various types of bugs, such as critical, high, medium, and low-severity vulnerabilities. Understand the reward structures and prioritize hunting for critical vulnerabilities.

6. Communication Channels:

Bug bounty platforms provide communication channels to interact with organizations and their security teams. Use these channels responsibly and professionally to discuss findings and clarify any issues.

7. Collaborative Approach:

Some platforms promote collaboration among ethical hackers. Participate in community discussions, share knowledge, and learn from experienced bug bounty hunters.

8. Timing and Persistence:

Bug bounty hunting requires patience and persistence. Stay consistent in your efforts, and continuously monitor the platform for new program announcements and updates.

9. Reports and Documentation:

When reporting vulnerabilities, provide clear and detailed reports with step-by-step instructions for reproducing the issue. Include evidence and PoCs (Proof of Concepts) to help organizations understand the impact and severity.

10. Responsible Disclosure:

Always adhere to responsible disclosure practices. Refrain from sharing or exploiting vulnerabilities beyond the platform and avoid causing harm or unauthorized access.

11. Continuous Learning:

Stay updated with the latest security trends, attack techniques, and emerging technologies. Continuous learning will enhance your skills and make you more effective in finding vulnerabilities.

12. Ethics and Professionalism:

Demonstrate ethical behavior and professionalism throughout your bug bounty journey. Respect the privacy and security of the target organizations and adhere to industry best practices.

Navigating bug bounty platforms requires a combination of technical skills, communication abilities, and a strong commitment to ethical hacking principles. By approaching bug bounty hunting with diligence, integrity, and a passion for cybersecurity, you can establish a successful and rewarding career in this field.

5.2 Target Selection and Scope Analysis

Target selection and scope analysis are crucial steps in bug bounty hunting. Choosing the right targets and understanding the scope of bug bounty programs can significantly impact your success as an ethical hacker. Here are some key considerations for target selection and scope analysis:

1. Understanding Your Expertise:

Start by evaluating your own strengths and expertise in different areas of cybersecurity. Focus on targets that align with your skills, whether it's web applications, mobile apps, IoT devices, network infrastructure, or specific programming languages.

2. Researching Bug Bounty Programs:

Thoroughly research bug bounty platforms to identify programs that match your skills and interests. Review the different programs' rules, rewards, and previous reported vulnerabilities to assess their compatibility with your capabilities.

3. Assessing Target Reputation:

Evaluate the reputation and track record of the target organization. Established companies or organizations with a history of running successful bug bounty programs are generally more reliable and responsive.

4. Scoping Constraints:

Pay close attention to the program's scope, which defines what assets and vulnerabilities are eligible for rewards. Some programs may focus on specific subdomains, applications, or components. Understand the limitations and boundaries of the target.

5. Legal and Ethical Considerations:

Ensure that your bug bounty hunting activities align with legal and ethical guidelines. Verify that the target organization has authorized the testing, and strictly adhere to the program's rules and disclosure policies.

6. Identifying Critical Assets:

Identify the most critical assets or components of the target organization. These may include high-value web applications, databases, customer portals, payment systems, or infrastructure elements.

7. Testing Environments:

Check if the target organization provides dedicated testing environments or staging environments for ethical hackers. Understand which environments are in scope and avoid testing on production systems.

8. Types of Vulnerabilities:

Analyze the types of vulnerabilities the program is interested in. Some programs may prioritize high-impact vulnerabilities like Remote Code Execution (RCE) or SQL Injection, while others may focus on specific bug classes.

9. Avoiding Low-Impact Targets:

While hunting for low-impact vulnerabilities can be a good learning experience, prioritize targets that offer significant rewards for high-impact findings. This allows you to maximize your efforts and potential earnings.

10. Continuous Program Monitoring:

Regularly monitor bug bounty platforms for new programs or updates to existing ones. New programs may present unique opportunities or offer attractive rewards for your expertise.

11. Feedback and Communication:

Engage with the target organization's security team if possible. Seek clarification on the scope, ask questions, and request feedback on your submissions to improve your skills.

By conducting a thorough analysis of the target and its scope, ethical hackers can focus their efforts on high-potential opportunities and optimize their bug bounty hunting strategy. Remember that success in bug bounty hunting requires a combination of technical skills, persistence, and a responsible approach to finding and reporting vulnerabilities.

5.3 Bug Bounty Hunting Methodologies

Bug bounty hunting methodologies provide a systematic approach for ethical hackers to efficiently and effectively search for vulnerabilities in target systems. While individual methodologies may vary, most bug bounty hunters follow a structured process to organize their testing efforts. Here is a general bug bounty hunting methodology:

1. Reconnaissance:

Gather information about the target organization, its assets, and web presence. Use open-source intelligence (OSINT) techniques to find subdomains, IP ranges, and other potential entry points.

2. Scanning and Enumeration:

Conduct network scanning and enumeration to identify active hosts, open ports, and services. Use tools like Nmap and Nessus to discover potential vulnerabilities.

3. Web Application Testing:

Focus on web application security testing. Analyze the target's web applications for common vulnerabilities like XSS, SQLi, CSRF, and insecure direct object references (IDOR).

4. Mobile Application Testing (If Applicable):

If the target includes mobile applications, perform security testing to identify vulnerabilities specific to mobile platforms, such as insecure data storage or communication.

5. IoT and OT Testing (If Applicable):

For IoT and OT targets, probe for weaknesses in the device firmware, communication protocols, and access controls.

6. Exploitation and Post-Exploitation (With Authorization):

After identifying vulnerabilities, attempt to exploit them with proper authorization. Gain unauthorized access to showcase the potential impact of the security flaws.

7. Documentation and Reporting:

Create detailed reports for each identified vulnerability, including steps to reproduce, potential impact, and recommended mitigations. Use proof of concepts (PoCs) to illustrate the vulnerabilities.

8. Responsible Disclosure:

Follow responsible disclosure practices when reporting vulnerabilities to the target organization. Give them adequate time to address the issues before public disclosure.

9. Collaboration and Community Engagement:

Engage with other bug bounty hunters and security professionals in the bug bounty community. Collaborate on challenges, share knowledge, and learn from others' experiences.

10. Continuous Learning and Adaptation:

Stay updated with the latest security trends, tools, and attack techniques. Continuously learn and adapt your bug bounty hunting approach to tackle new challenges effectively.

11. Time Management:

Allocate time efficiently for different phases of bug bounty hunting. Balance recon, scanning, testing, and reporting to maximize productivity.

12. Persistence and Patience:

Bug bounty hunting can be a challenging process that requires perseverance. Be patient and persistent in your efforts to discover vulnerabilities.

Remember that bug bounty hunting is a responsible and ethical practice. Always obtain proper authorization from the target organization before conducting any testing, and adhere to the platform's rules and guidelines. Ethical hacking is not about causing harm or disrupting systems; it's about helping organizations improve their security by identifying and mitigating vulnerabilities before malicious actors exploit them.

5.4 Maximizing Efficiency with Automation Tools

Maximizing efficiency with automation tools is a key strategy for bug bounty hunters to enhance their productivity and effectiveness. Automation can help streamline repetitive tasks, perform large-scale scanning, and identify common vulnerabilities quickly. Here are some automation tools that bug bounty hunters can leverage to improve their efficiency:

1. Reconnaissance and Information Gathering:

- **Sublist3r and Subfinder**: Automated subdomain enumeration tools that help identify subdomains associated with the target organization.
- **Amass**: A versatile tool for DNS enumeration, subdomain discovery, and network mapping.
- **theHarvester**: Automates the gathering of emails, subdomains, and other information related to the target organization.

2. Scanning and Vulnerability Assessment:

- **Nmap**: A powerful network scanning tool that can perform host discovery, port scanning, version detection, and OS fingerprinting.
- **Nessus and OpenVAS**: Automated vulnerability scanners that can identify known vulnerabilities in target systems and applications.
- **Burp Suite Professional**: An integrated platform for web application security testing, including scanning for common web vulnerabilities.

3. Web Application Security Testing:

- **OWASP ZAP (Zed Attack Proxy):** A widely used web application security scanner and testing tool.
- **SQLMap**: A tool for automating SQL injection detection and exploitation in web applications.

4. Exploitation and Post-Exploitation:

- **Metasploit Framework**: An extensive penetration testing tool that includes a vast collection of exploits for various systems and applications.
- **Empire**: A post-exploitation framework for Windows, macOS, and Linux systems that enables various privilege escalation and lateral movement techniques.

5. Reporting and Documentation:

- **Dradis Framework**: A collaboration and reporting tool that allows bug bounty hunters to manage and document their findings effectively.
- **Markdown and Templates**: Create custom reporting templates in Markdown or use existing templates to structure vulnerability reports efficiently.

6. Continuous Monitoring:

- **Security Information and Event Management (SIEM) Tools**: Leverage SIEM solutions to automate the monitoring of security events and logs from various sources.
- **Custom Scripts and Cron Jobs**: Develop custom scripts to automate periodic scanning and monitoring tasks.

7. Collaboration and Communication:

- **Slack and Discord Bots**: Integrate bots that provide real-time updates on bug bounty programs, new submissions, or community discussions.
- **GitHub and GitLab Integrations**: Use integrations to automate the tracking and management of bug bounty-related repositories and submissions.

It's essential to use automation tools responsibly and ethically, following the rules and guidelines set by bug bounty platforms and the target organization. Automation should enhance the bug bounty hunter's capabilities, but human judgment and validation remain critical to ensure accurate and reliable results. Continuous learning and adaptation are essential to staying updated with the latest automation tools and techniques, maximizing their benefits in the bug bounty hunting process.

Chapter 6: Reporting Bugs Effectively

In the realm of bug bounty hunting, the discovery of vulnerabilities marks only the beginning of a bug hunter's journey. Welcome to Chapter 6 of "Bug Bounty Unleashed: Mastering the Art of Ethical Hacking and Rewards." In this chapter, we delve into the crucial process of reporting bugs effectively—a skill that distinguishes exceptional bug hunters and fosters productive collaborations with program owners.

Crafting Comprehensive Bug Reports

Effective bug reports are the cornerstone of successful bug bounty hunting. In this section, we guide you through the elements of a well-structured bug report, including clear vulnerability descriptions, step-by-step replication instructions, and supporting evidence. By mastering the art of crafting comprehensive bug reports, you will communicate your findings succinctly and facilitate program owners' understanding of the issue.

Communicating with Program Owners

Building strong communication channels with program owners is vital for successful collaboration. We explore the significance of open and transparent communication in sharing your findings responsibly. By fostering a constructive dialogue, you will work closely with program owners to ensure they grasp the severity of the vulnerability and the steps needed for remediation.

Proof-of-Concept Demonstrations

Verifying the existence of vulnerabilities through proof-of-concept (PoC) demonstrations is a crucial step in the reporting process. We provide insights into creating effective PoCs that illustrate the impact of discovered vulnerabilities without causing harm. By mastering the art of PoC demonstrations, you will instill confidence in program owners and facilitate faster remediation.

Responsible Disclosure and Coordinated Vulnerability Disclosure (CVD)

Ethical hackers play a vital role in responsible disclosure—the process of notifying affected parties of vulnerabilities in a responsible manner. We explore the principles of responsible disclosure and discuss the importance of adhering to Coordinated Vulnerability Disclosure (CVD) policies. By following these ethical guidelines, you will uphold the highest standards of professional conduct in the bug bounty community.

Acknowledging and Handling Duplicate Reports

Duplicate reports are an inherent aspect of bug bounty hunting. Understanding how to handle them responsibly and graciously is essential for maintaining a positive reputation. In this section, we discuss strategies for acknowledging and collaborating with other hunters who might have identified the same vulnerabilities. By fostering a collaborative atmosphere, you contribute to a thriving bug bounty community.

Leveraging Responsible Disclosure Platforms

In the interconnected world of bug bounty hunting, responsible disclosure platforms provide bug hunters with secure channels to communicate findings responsibly. We introduce you to platforms like Open Bug Bounty and CERT/CC, highlighting their significance in responsible vulnerability disclosure. By leveraging these platforms, you contribute to a safer digital ecosystem while furthering your bug bounty hunting journey.

Impactful Reports: Beyond the Bounty

As this chapter concludes, we remind you that impactful bug reports extend beyond the monetary rewards they may yield. Your contributions to securing digital systems, your professionalism, and your dedication to responsible disclosure shape your identity as a skilled and trusted bug hunter. Through your reports, you leave a lasting impact on the security posture of organizations and the larger cybersecurity community.

By mastering the art of reporting bugs effectively, you become a beacon of professionalism and integrity in the bug bounty hunting landscape. Your contributions will be valued, respected, and rewarded, further motivating you to embark on even greater ethical hacking endeavors.

6.1 Crafting Comprehensive Bug Reports

Crafting comprehensive bug reports is crucial for bug bounty hunters to communicate their findings effectively to the target organization's security team. A well-written bug report helps the organization understand the identified vulnerability clearly and enables them to take appropriate action to fix the issue. Here are the key elements of crafting a comprehensive bug report:

1. Clear and Descriptive Title:

The title should succinctly describe the nature of the vulnerability. Avoid vague titles and include keywords related to the vulnerability type.

2. Executive Summary:

Provide a brief overview of the vulnerability, its potential impact, and affected assets. The executive summary allows readers to grasp the severity of the issue quickly.

3. Vulnerability Description:

Clearly explain the nature of the vulnerability, including the steps to reproduce it and the attack scenario. Use step-by-step instructions and include relevant screenshots or code snippets to illustrate the vulnerability.

4. Impact and Severity Assessment:

Assess the potential impact of the vulnerability and its severity level. Use a standardized severity rating (e.g., CVSS score) if available.

5. Proof of Concept (PoC):

Include a detailed PoC that demonstrates the vulnerability in action. The PoC should be easily reproducible by the target organization's security team.

6. Affected Components and Systems:

Specify the components, versions, and systems affected by the vulnerability. This helps the organization understand the scope of the issue.

7. Steps to Remediate:

Suggest possible mitigation or remediation steps to fix the vulnerability. Provide guidance or code snippets, if applicable, to assist with the remediation process.

8. Attach Supporting Materials:

Include any relevant log files, request/response data, or additional information that supports the findings. This additional data aids in the organization's validation and resolution process.

9. References and Related Information:

Provide references to relevant resources, such as vulnerability databases, security advisories, or industry standards related to the identified vulnerability.

10. Responsible Disclosure Agreement:

Confirm that you will adhere to the organization's responsible disclosure policy and refrain from publicly disclosing the vulnerability until the organization has had sufficient time to address it.

11. Timely Submission:

Submit the bug report as soon as possible after identifying the vulnerability. Prompt submission allows the organization to address the issue promptly and prevent potential exploits.

12. Professional Tone and Language:

Write the report using a professional and respectful tone. Avoid confrontational language and focus on conveying the technical details clearly.

Remember that the goal of a bug report is to help the organization understand and fix the vulnerability effectively. Provide sufficient details, but avoid overwhelming the reader with unnecessary information. Craft the report with clarity, precision, and a focus on impact to ensure that the organization can address the vulnerability efficiently and enhance their security posture.

6.2 Communicating with Program Owners

Effective communication with program owners is a critical aspect of bug bounty hunting. Building a positive rapport and conveying your findings clearly can lead to a more productive and rewarding experience. Here are some tips for communicating with program owners:

1. Be Professional and Courteous:

Maintain a professional and courteous tone in all communications. Treat program owners with respect and understanding.

2. Follow Program Guidelines:

Adhere to the bug bounty program's rules, guidelines, and disclosure policies. Ensure that you are within the scope and boundaries defined by the program.

3. Use the Right Channels:

Use the designated channels provided by the bug bounty platform or the program owner to communicate. Avoid contacting program owners through personal or unapproved means.

4. Provide Clear and Detailed Reports:

Submit well-written and comprehensive bug reports that clearly outline the identified vulnerabilities, their impact, and steps to reproduce them. Include screenshots, PoCs, and any relevant evidence.

5. Focus on Impact:

Emphasize the potential impact of the vulnerability rather than just its technical details. Explain how the vulnerability could be exploited and the risks it poses to the organization.

6. Be Timely in Your Communications:

Respond to program owners promptly, especially if they ask for additional information or clarifications. Timely communication demonstrates your commitment to the bug bounty process.

7. Be Patient and Understanding:

Understand that program owners may receive numerous reports and have other responsibilities. Be patient and give them reasonable time to review and respond to your findings.

8. Be Open to Feedback:

Be receptive to feedback from program owners. If they request additional information or ask for clarifications, respond in a cooperative manner.

9. Respect Confidentiality and Disclosure Policies:

Do not share any sensitive information or details of your findings with others, unless explicitly allowed by the program owner's disclosure policy.

10. Keep Communications Private:

Avoid discussing the details of your findings or communications with the program owner in public forums or with others who are not directly involved in the bug bounty process.

11. Report Ethical Concerns:

If you come across any ethical concerns or potential issues with the bug bounty program or the organization's security practices, report them privately to the program owner or the bug bounty platform.

12. Seek Clarifications Professionally:

If you have any doubts or need clarifications about the program's scope or rules, ask the program owner professionally for guidance.

By maintaining open, professional, and respectful communication with program owners, you can foster a positive working relationship that benefits both you as a bug bounty hunter and the organization running the program. Effective communication helps program owners understand the value of your findings and encourages them to address the identified vulnerabilities promptly, enhancing the overall security of the organization's systems and applications.

6.3 Proof-of-Concept Demonstrations

Proof-of-Concept (PoC) demonstrations are an essential part of bug bounty reports. A PoC is a practical illustration of the identified vulnerability, showcasing how it can be exploited. Including a clear and effective PoC in your bug report helps program owners understand the severity of the issue and validates the authenticity of your findings. Here are some tips for creating impactful PoC demonstrations:

1. Reproducibility:

Ensure that your PoC is easily reproducible by the program owner's security team. Provide step-by-step instructions, including the necessary tools and payloads used.

2. Keep It Simple:

Aim for simplicity in your PoC. A concise and straightforward demonstration makes it easier for the program owner to grasp the vulnerability and its impact.

3. Avoid Destructive Actions:

Your PoC should not cause any harm or damage to the target system. Avoid performing actions that could disrupt or compromise the system's integrity.

4. Focus on Impact:

Emphasize the potential consequences of the vulnerability in your PoC. Show how an attacker could exploit it to gain unauthorized access or compromise sensitive data.

5. Use Realistic Scenarios:

Create PoC demonstrations that align with real-world attack scenarios. Program owners appreciate PoCs that mirror practical threats to their systems.

6. Include Relevant Code Snippets:

If your PoC involves any code, include relevant snippets in your report. Explain the purpose and function of the code to help the program owner understand its significance.

7. Capture Screenshots or Videos:

Visual aids can enhance the clarity of your PoC. Capture screenshots or create short videos demonstrating the steps of the exploit.

8. Anonymize or Redact Sensitive Data:

If your PoC includes any sensitive data from the target system, ensure that you anonymize or redact it before including it in the report.

9. Test in a Controlled Environment:

Conduct your PoC demonstrations in a controlled environment or the testing environment provided by the bug bounty program. Avoid testing on production systems.

10. Provide Clear Context:

Precede your PoC with a clear explanation of the vulnerability and its impact. This context helps the program owner understand the significance of the demonstration.

11. Test Edge Cases:

If applicable, test edge cases or unusual scenarios in your PoC. Sometimes vulnerabilities manifest only under specific conditions.

12. Mention Limitations:

Acknowledge any limitations or constraints in your PoC. If the exploit requires certain conditions to be met, mention them to set realistic expectations.

An effective PoC is a powerful tool that reinforces the severity of your findings and enhances the credibility of your bug bounty report. By presenting your discoveries in a clear, concise, and impactful manner, you increase the chances of receiving appropriate recognition and rewards for your efforts.

6.4 Responsible Disclosure and Coordinated Vulnerability Disclosure (CVD)

Responsible Disclosure and Coordinated Vulnerability Disclosure (CVD) are practices followed by ethical hackers and security researchers when reporting vulnerabilities to organizations. These practices aim to balance the need for security with the protection of end-users, customers, and the organization's reputation. Here's a breakdown of both concepts:

1. Responsible Disclosure:

Responsible Disclosure is the process of reporting security vulnerabilities to the affected organization in a responsible and ethical manner. When a security researcher or bug bounty hunter discovers a vulnerability, they follow these steps:

- **Verify the Vulnerability**: Confirm that the identified vulnerability is legitimate and not a false positive.
- **Notify the Organization**: Contact the organization's security team or designated

point of contact to report the vulnerability privately and securely.

- **Provide Adequate Details**: Include clear and comprehensive information about the vulnerability, its impact, and steps to reproduce it (a PoC).
- **Set a Disclosure Timeline**: Allow the organization a reasonable amount of time to address the vulnerability before disclosing it publicly. The time frame is usually agreed upon between the researcher and the organization.
- **Keep the Vulnerability Confidential**: Maintain the confidentiality of the vulnerability until it has been resolved or the agreed-upon disclosure timeline has passed.
- **Public Disclosure (If Necessary):** If the organization fails to address the vulnerability within the agreed-upon timeline, the researcher may consider public disclosure as a last resort. Public disclosure aims to pressure the organization to fix the vulnerability and protect end-users.

2. Coordinated Vulnerability Disclosure (CVD):

Coordinated Vulnerability Disclosure (CVD) is a collaborative approach to reporting and resolving security vulnerabilities. It involves coordinated efforts between the security researcher, the affected organization, and sometimes other stakeholders like vendors or CERT (Computer Emergency Response

Team). The steps in CVD are similar to responsible disclosure:

- **Discovery and Verification**: The researcher identifies and verifies the vulnerability.
- **Contact the Vendor/Organization**: The researcher privately contacts the vendor or organization affected by the vulnerability.
- **Coordinate Efforts**: The researcher and the vendor work together to understand the vulnerability, assess its impact, and determine mitigation steps.
- **Vendor Remediation**: The vendor develops and tests a security patch or fix for the vulnerability.
- **Release of Patch and Public Disclosure**: Once the vendor releases the patch or fix, the researcher and the vendor coordinate the public disclosure of the vulnerability and the corresponding patch.

CVD emphasizes cooperation and collaboration between the security community and organizations to improve cybersecurity and protect end-users. It recognizes that both researchers and organizations have a shared interest in maintaining a secure digital environment.

Adhering to responsible disclosure and CVD practices ensures that vulnerabilities are addressed promptly and responsibly, reducing the risk of potential exploits and harm to users. It also encourages a more positive and constructive relationship between security researchers and organizations, fostering a safer online ecosystem for everyone.

Chapter 7: Responsible Disclosure and Legal Considerations

In the ever-evolving landscape of bug bounty hunting, ethical hackers must navigate the delicate balance between uncovering vulnerabilities and responsibly disclosing them. Welcome to Chapter 7 of "Bug Bounty Unleashed: Mastering the Art of Ethical Hacking and Rewards." In this chapter, we delve into the ethical and legal dimensions of responsible vulnerability disclosure, empowering you to uphold the highest standards of professional conduct.

The Ethics of Responsible Disclosure

Responsible disclosure is rooted in the ethical obligation of ethical hackers to protect digital systems and user data. In this section, we explore the core principles of responsible disclosure, emphasizing the importance of acting in good faith and prioritizing users' safety. By understanding the ethical underpinnings, you will become a responsible guardian of cybersecurity, ensuring that vulnerabilities are addressed with integrity and transparency.

Legal Considerations for Bug Hunters

As an ethical hacker, you operate in a legal landscape that requires careful consideration of potential risks and liabilities. In this segment, we discuss the legal aspects of bug hunting, including the Computer Fraud and Abuse Act (CFAA), the Digital Millennium Copyright Act (DMCA), and international legal frameworks. By understanding these legal considerations, you will navigate the bug bounty hunting landscape responsibly and protect yourself from inadvertent legal repercussions.

Understanding Bug Bounty Policies and Agreements

Bug bounty programs often have distinct policies and agreements that govern how ethical hackers interact with their platforms and the organizations they serve. We explore the nuances of program policies, vulnerability disclosure agreements (VDAs), and legal terms of engagement. By familiarizing yourself with these policies, you will participate in bug bounty programs confidently and responsibly.

Navigating Non-Disclosure Agreements (NDAs)

Non-Disclosure Agreements (NDAs) are common in the bug bounty landscape, especially when dealing with pre-disclosure or coordinated disclosure processes. In this section, we discuss the intricacies of NDAs, including the restrictions they impose and their duration. By navigating NDAs with prudence, you will foster constructive relationships with program owners and comply with their disclosure requirements.

The Role of Coordinated Vulnerability Disclosure (CVD)

Coordinated Vulnerability Disclosure (CVD) is a collaborative approach that brings together ethical hackers, program owners, and affected parties in a controlled disclosure process. We explore the significance of CVD in responsible vulnerability disclosure, ensuring that vulnerabilities are patched without unnecessarily exposing users to risk. By adhering to CVD principles, you contribute to a harmonious and efficient vulnerability remediation process.

The Importance of Confidentiality

Confidentiality is a cornerstone of responsible disclosure. In this segment, we underscore the significance of maintaining strict confidentiality while investigating and reporting vulnerabilities. By respecting the confidentiality of information shared by program owners, you demonstrate professionalism and reliability in your bug hunting pursuits.

In the realm of responsible disclosure and legal considerations, ethical hackers play a vital role in safeguarding the digital world. By upholding ethical principles, complying with legal requirements, and fostering constructive collaborations with program owners, you contribute to a secure cyberspace that protects the interests of organizations and users alike.

As this chapter concludes, remember that your ethical conduct extends beyond the boundaries of hacking exploits—it reflects your commitment to a safer and more resilient digital ecosystem. Embrace the responsibilities that come with being an ethical hacker, and let your actions pave the way for a more secure and trustworthy cyber landscape.

7.1 The Ethics of Responsible Disclosure

The ethics of responsible disclosure are fundamental principles that guide the actions of security researchers, bug bounty hunters, and ethical hackers when reporting vulnerabilities to organizations. Responsible disclosure aims to strike a balance between promoting cybersecurity and protecting the interests of affected parties. The key ethical considerations in responsible disclosure include:

1. Minimizing Harm:

The primary ethical consideration in responsible disclosure is to minimize harm to users and organizations. Researchers should avoid publicly disclosing vulnerabilities before a patch is available, as it could lead to malicious exploitation.

2. Confidentiality and Trust:

Ethical hackers must respect the confidentiality of the vulnerability until it has been appropriately addressed by the organization. This builds trust between researchers and organizations, fostering better cooperation in the future.

3. Respect for User Privacy:

Responsible disclosure involves safeguarding the privacy and data of users affected by the vulnerability. Researchers should avoid accessing or manipulating user data beyond what is necessary to demonstrate the vulnerability's impact.

4. Cooperation with Organizations:

Ethical hackers should actively cooperate with organizations during the disclosure process. This includes providing sufficient information, maintaining open communication, and allowing organizations reasonable time to fix the issue.

5. Non-Disclosure Agreements (NDAs):

Some organizations may request researchers to sign NDAs (Non-Disclosure Agreements) to protect sensitive information. Researchers should honor these agreements and refrain from disclosing information without permission.

6. Impact Assessment:

Ethical hackers should accurately assess the potential impact of the vulnerability. High-severity vulnerabilities may require expedited disclosure, whereas low-severity issues might allow more time for remediation.

7. Responsible Public Disclosure (If Necessary):

If an organization fails to respond or fix a vulnerability within a reasonable timeframe, researchers may consider responsible public disclosure. However, this should be a last resort and undertaken with care to avoid unnecessary risks.

8. Avoiding Extortion or Blackmail:

Ethical hackers must never use the threat of public disclosure to extort organizations for financial gain or other benefits. Such actions are unethical and may lead to legal consequences.

9. No Unauthorized Access:

Responsible disclosure does not justify unauthorized access to systems or data beyond what is necessary to identify and verify the vulnerability.

10. Cultural Sensitivity:

Researchers should be mindful of the cultural and legal context of the organization they are dealing with. What may be acceptable in one culture might be viewed differently in another.

Adhering to these ethical principles promotes a safer digital environment and fosters positive collaboration between ethical hackers and organizations. Responsible disclosure ensures that vulnerabilities are addressed promptly, ultimately benefiting the security and privacy of users and organizations alike.

7.2 Legal Considerations for Bug Hunters

Legal considerations are of paramount importance for bug hunters, as they engage in activities that involve testing and potentially accessing systems that do not belong to them. While bug hunting is an essential practice for improving cybersecurity, ethical hackers must be aware of the legal boundaries and potential risks involved. Here are some key legal considerations for bug hunters:

1. Authorization:

Always obtain explicit written permission or join authorized bug bounty programs before testing or assessing any system. Unauthorized access to systems is illegal and may lead to severe legal consequences.

2. Scope Limitations:

Respect the defined scope of the bug bounty program or authorization. Testing outside the agreed-upon scope might lead to unintended consequences and legal repercussions.

3. Terms of Service and Policies:

Review and understand the organization's terms of service, acceptable use policies, and bug bounty guidelines. Adherence to these policies is crucial to staying within legal boundaries.

4. Responsible Disclosure:

Follow the principles of responsible disclosure and coordinated vulnerability disclosure (CVD). Avoid public disclosure of vulnerabilities before the organization has had an opportunity to address them.

5. Privacy and Data Protection Laws:

Be aware of the privacy and data protection laws in the countries where the organization operates. Avoid accessing or disclosing sensitive user data without proper authorization.

6. Cybercrime Laws and Computer Fraud Acts:

Understand the relevant cybercrime laws and computer fraud acts in your jurisdiction and the jurisdiction of the organization. Unlawful actions could lead to criminal charges.

7. Non-Disclosure Agreements (NDAs):

If you sign an NDA (Non-Disclosure Agreement) with the organization, ensure that you strictly adhere to its terms to avoid potential legal conflicts.

8. Intellectual Property Rights:

Respect the intellectual property rights of the organization. Do not reproduce or share proprietary information without explicit permission.

9. User Consent:

If your bug hunting activities involve interactions with users or user data, obtain informed consent from the affected users, where applicable.

10. Record Keeping:

Maintain detailed records of your bug hunting activities, communications with the organization, and any agreements or permissions obtained.

11. Consult Legal Counsel:

If you are uncertain about the legal implications of your bug hunting activities, consider seeking advice from legal counsel specializing in cybersecurity and information technology law.

12. Reporting Security Incidents:

If you accidentally cause any security incidents or disruptions during your bug hunting, promptly report them to the organization so that they can take appropriate actions.

By being mindful of these legal considerations, bug hunters can ensure that their activities are conducted responsibly, ethically, and within the boundaries of the law. Responsible bug hunting plays a vital role in improving cybersecurity, and compliance with legal requirements ensures that this valuable practice can continue to benefit both organizations and the wider digital community.

7.3 Understanding Bug Bounty Policies and Agreements

Understanding bug bounty policies and agreements is essential for bug hunters to participate in bug bounty programs responsibly and effectively. These policies and agreements outline the rules, scope, rewards, and expectations for bug hunting activities within a specific program. Here's what bug hunters should understand about bug bounty policies and agreements:

1. Scope of the Program:

The bug bounty program's scope defines which assets, applications, and systems are eligible for testing. It is essential to know the program's scope to avoid testing unauthorized areas.

2. Vulnerabilities in Scope:

Bug bounty policies typically list the types of vulnerabilities that are eligible for rewards. Focus on finding vulnerabilities that are within the program's accepted categories.

3. Vulnerabilities Out of Scope:

Conversely, the policies also mention the vulnerabilities that are out of scope and not eligible for rewards. Avoid testing such areas to prevent potential negative consequences.

4. Rules and Guidelines:

Bug bounty programs have specific rules and guidelines that participants must follow. These may include rules on disclosure, reporting formats, testing times, and restrictions on certain testing techniques.

5. Reporting Process:

Understand the reporting process for the bug bounty program. This includes how to submit bug reports, what information to include, and how to communicate with the program owners.

6. Responsible Disclosure Period:

Some programs require a responsible disclosure period during which the researcher must wait before public disclosure. Comply with this period to give the organization time to address the vulnerability.

7. Non-Disclosure Agreements (NDAs):

Some bug bounty programs may require researchers to sign NDAs to protect sensitive information. Be aware of any NDAs and adhere to their terms.

8. Rewards and Recognition:

Familiarize yourself with the reward structure and the criteria for earning rewards. Understand how the program owner determines the severity of a vulnerability and the corresponding payout.

9. Duplicate Submissions:

Bug bounty policies usually address how duplicate submissions are handled. Avoid submitting reports for vulnerabilities that have already been reported by others.

10. Legal Implications:

Bug bounty agreements may include clauses that specify the legal implications of violating the program's policies or engaging in unauthorized activities. Comply with these terms to avoid legal issues.

11. Program Changes and Updates:

Be aware that bug bounty programs can undergo changes or updates over time. Keep yourself informed about any modifications to the program's policies or scope.

12. Communication Channels:

Identify the appropriate communication channels for interacting with the program owners and other participants. Follow the program's guidelines for communication.

Understanding bug bounty policies and agreements is crucial for maintaining a positive relationship with program owners and ensuring that your bug hunting activities align with ethical and legal standards. By adhering to the program's guidelines and communicating effectively, bug hunters can contribute to a safer digital environment and be rewarded for their responsible efforts.

7.4 Navigating Non-Disclosure Agreements (NDAs)

Navigating Non-Disclosure Agreements (NDAs) is a critical aspect of bug hunting, especially when participating in bug bounty programs or engaging in security research. NDAs are legal contracts that impose confidentiality obligations on the involved parties, and understanding and complying with them is essential to avoid potential legal issues. Here's how bug hunters can navigate NDAs effectively:

1. Read Carefully Before Signing:

Thoroughly read and understand the NDA before signing it. Pay attention to the scope of confidentiality, the duration of the agreement, and any specific requirements or restrictions.

2. Seek Legal Advice if Uncertain:

If you are unsure about any provisions in the NDA, consider seeking advice from legal counsel experienced in cybersecurity and contract law. This will help ensure you fully understand your obligations.

3. Comply with Confidentiality Requirements:

Adhere strictly to the confidentiality requirements specified in the NDA. Avoid sharing any sensitive information covered by the agreement with unauthorized parties.

4. Report Vulnerabilities Confidentially:

When participating in a bug bounty program or responsible disclosure, submit vulnerability reports confidentially through the designated channels outlined in the program's guidelines.

5. Limit Sharing of Information:

Restrict access to information covered by the NDA to only those who need to know. Avoid discussing confidential details with colleagues or friends who are not involved in the bug bounty or research.

6. Mark and Label Confidential Information:

Clearly mark any information that falls under the NDA as "Confidential" to ensure that its status is evident to anyone who may handle the information.

7. Be Cautious with Public Statements:

Avoid making public statements or disclosures that might violate the NDA. This includes sharing information about the organization, its systems, or the vulnerabilities identified.

8. Seek Permission for Public Disclosures:

If you believe a vulnerability deserves public disclosure, request permission from the program owner or organization covered by the NDA before making any public statements.

9. Handle Information Securely:

Securely store and transmit any confidential information received during bug hunting or security research. Use encryption and other security measures as appropriate.

10. Maintain Records:

Keep records of all communications and activities related to the bug bounty program or security research, including interactions with program owners and any agreements made.

11. Comply with NDA Termination:

If the NDA has an expiration or termination clause, ensure that you comply with its terms. Stop accessing or using confidential information once the NDA is no longer in effect.

12. Report Violations Promptly:

If you suspect a potential violation of the NDA, report it to the appropriate party promptly. Reporting violations is essential to protect the interests of all parties involved.

Navigating NDAs with integrity and compliance is vital to maintaining a professional and ethical approach to bug hunting and security research. Respecting confidentiality agreements establishes trust between bug hunters and organizations, fostering a collaborative environment for improving cybersecurity responsibly.

Chapter 8: Challenges and Lessons from Real-Life Bug Bounties

In the world of bug bounty hunting, every discovery presents its own set of challenges and learning opportunities. Welcome to Chapter 8 of "Bug Bounty Unleashed: Mastering the Art of Ethical Hacking and Rewards." In this chapter, we delve into real-life bug bounty experiences, exploring the challenges faced by bug hunters and the valuable lessons garnered from their successes and setbacks.

Case Studies of Successful Bug Hunters

In this section, we present compelling case studies of successful bug hunters who have achieved remarkable feats in the bug bounty landscape. By analyzing their methodologies, tactics, and the vulnerabilities they uncovered, you will gain insights into the strategies that have proven effective in real-world scenarios. Drawing inspiration from these case studies, you will be motivated to apply similar approaches in your bug hunting endeavors.

Analyzing High-Profile Bug Bounty Payouts

High-profile bug bounty payouts capture the imagination of the bug hunting community, showcasing the immense rewards awaiting skilled hunters. We delve into these success stories, understanding the magnitude of their impact on organizations and cybersecurity as a whole. By analyzing these cases, you will grasp the potential rewards for your efforts and the immense value ethical hackers bring to the digital world.

Learning from Bug Bounty Failures

In the pursuit of excellence, bug hunters may encounter challenges and occasional failures. In this segment, we explore instances where bug hunters faced setbacks and vulnerabilities eluded their discovery. By understanding the lessons learned from these experiences, you will gain a resilient mindset, adapting your strategies to overcome obstacles and continue your bug hunting journey with determination.

Strategies for Overcoming Common Challenges

Every bug hunting expedition presents its share of challenges, such as limited program scopes, low signal-to-noise ratios, and the constant evolution of attack surfaces. We discuss effective strategies to overcome these common challenges, from enhancing your reconnaissance skills to collaborating with program owners to expand program scopes. By embracing these strategies, you will optimize your bug hunting efforts and yield more impactful results.

In the diverse and dynamic world of bug bounty hunting, challenges and lessons are the building blocks of growth and expertise. As you journey through the experiences of successful bug hunters and analyze the outcomes of their endeavors, you will be inspired to approach your bug hunting pursuits with tenacity, creativity, and a relentless pursuit of knowledge.

Remember, the pursuit of excellence is not defined solely by successes, but also by the lessons learned from setbacks. Embrace the challenges and seize the opportunities presented in real-life bug bounties, for they are the stepping stones to becoming a proficient and respected bug bounty hunter.

8.1 Case Studies of Successful Bug Hunters

While I don't have access to real-time data or specific case studies beyond my last knowledge update in September 2021, I can provide you with some examples of successful bug hunters up to that date. These bug hunters have made significant contributions to improving cybersecurity through responsible vulnerability disclosure and ethical hacking. Keep in mind that bug hunting is an ongoing practice, and many other bug hunters have likely made significant achievements beyond my last update. Here are a few examples:

1. Santiago Lopez (aka @try_to_hack):

Santiago Lopez, a young ethical hacker from Argentina, gained recognition as the first hacker to earn over $1 million in bug bounties on the HackerOne platform. He discovered vulnerabilities in systems for numerous high-profile companies.

2. Mark Litchfield (aka @mlitchfield):

Mark Litchfield is a renowned bug hunter and security researcher known for his exceptional contributions to the bug bounty community. He has discovered critical vulnerabilities in products and services of major organizations.

3. Frans Rosén (aka @fransrosen):

Frans Rosén is a prominent bug hunter and security consultant who has reported critical vulnerabilities to companies like Google, Facebook, and Apple. He is actively involved in responsible disclosure and sharing knowledge with the community.

4. Alex Birsan (aka @alxbrsn):

Alex Birsan is a skilled bug hunter known for his groundbreaking research on supply chain attacks. He uncovered a series of vulnerabilities by exploiting the software supply chain, earning him recognition and accolades from the cybersecurity community.

5. James Kettle (aka @albinowax):

James Kettle is a renowned bug hunter and the head of research at PortSwigger Web Security. He is well-known for his work on the Burp Suite web vulnerability scanner and has reported critical security flaws in various web applications.

6. Amal Bose (aka @amalbose1989):

Amal Bose is a proficient bug hunter who has made significant contributions to various bug bounty programs. He has discovered critical vulnerabilities in applications and services offered by top tech companies.

7. Tomasz Bojarski (aka @independentpl):

Tomasz Bojarski is an experienced bug hunter and security researcher with a strong track record in responsible disclosure. He has reported security flaws to major organizations and has been recognized for his expertise in web security.

Please note that these are just a few examples, and there are many other talented bug hunters who have contributed significantly to the cybersecurity community. Bug hunting is a collaborative effort, and these individuals, along with many others, have helped organizations enhance their security postures and protect users worldwide.

8.2 Analyzing High-Profile Bug Bounty Payouts

As of my last update in September 2021, high-profile bug bounty payouts have been an essential part of the bug hunting landscape. Companies offer significant rewards to incentivize ethical hackers and security researchers to find and responsibly disclose critical vulnerabilities in their systems. While specific payouts may vary based on the severity and impact of the vulnerabilities, here are some noteworthy examples of high-profile bug bounty payouts:

1. Apple Bug Bounty Program:

In 2021, Apple announced that it would offer a maximum bug bounty payout of $1.5 million for discovering vulnerabilities that could allow an attacker to gain full control of a user's device without user interaction.

2. Google Bug Bounty Program:

Google has one of the most well-known bug bounty programs, and it has rewarded researchers with substantial payouts. For instance, in 2021, Google paid out $31,337 for a critical bug found in Chrome.

3. Microsoft Bug Bounty Program:

Microsoft offers significant rewards for finding vulnerabilities in its products and services. In 2021, a researcher received $200,000 for discovering a new mitigation bypass technique.

4. Facebook Bug Bounty Program:

Facebook's bug bounty program is also known for its generous rewards. In the past, researchers have received substantial payouts for reporting critical vulnerabilities in Facebook's platform.

5. PayPal Bug Bounty Program:

PayPal is another company that places a high value on security. Researchers have been rewarded with sizable payouts for reporting vulnerabilities in PayPal's systems.

6. Tesla Bug Bounty Program:

Tesla, known for its electric vehicles, has offered impressive rewards for researchers who find and responsibly disclose security flaws in its systems.

7. GitHub Bug Bounty Program:

GitHub, the popular code repository platform, offers substantial rewards for reporting vulnerabilities affecting its services and infrastructure.

8. Intel Bug Bounty Program:

Intel, one of the leading semiconductor manufacturers, has a bug bounty program that offers rewards for finding vulnerabilities in its hardware and software products.

It's important to note that bug bounty payouts can vary significantly based on factors such as vulnerability severity, potential impact, and the company's own evaluation criteria. The examples mentioned above represent some of the well-known bug bounty programs, and the rewards offered may have evolved or changed since my last update. The bug bounty landscape is dynamic, with new programs and higher rewards continually emerging as companies prioritize cybersecurity and ethical hacking in safeguarding their systems and user data.

8.3 Learning from Bug Bounty Failures

Learning from bug bounty failures is a crucial aspect of improving the effectiveness and impact of bug hunting programs. Even experienced bug hunters and well-established companies can encounter challenges and mistakes during the bug hunting process. Analyzing these failures can provide valuable insights and lessons for bug hunters, organizations running bug bounty programs, and the broader cybersecurity community. Here are some key learning points from bug bounty failures:

1. Insufficient Scope Definition:

Bug bounty programs must have a clear and well-defined scope. Failures can occur when the scope is too broad or too narrow, leading to misunderstandings and misaligned expectations.

2. Poor Communication Channels:

Inadequate or inefficient communication channels between researchers and organizations can hinder the bug hunting process. Clear and open communication is essential for resolving issues promptly.

3. Lack of Vulnerability Severity Assessment:

Some bug bounty programs may fail to accurately assess the severity of reported vulnerabilities. This can lead to undervalued rewards or delayed fixes for critical issues.

4. Ignoring Valid Reports:

Organizations should avoid dismissing valid vulnerability reports without proper evaluation. Ignoring or underestimating the impact of a reported vulnerability can lead to potential exploitation.

5. Insufficient Rewards and Recognition:

Inadequate rewards or delayed recognition for successful bug hunters can discourage researchers from participating in a program or lead to reduced motivation.

6. Inconsistent Response Times:

Slow response times from organizations can frustrate researchers and hinder the timely resolution of vulnerabilities.

7. Lack of Program Evolution:

Bug bounty programs should evolve and adapt over time to address emerging threats and technologies. Failure to update program guidelines and rewards can result in reduced effectiveness.

8. Over Reliance on Automation:

Relying solely on automated tools for vulnerability detection may lead to false negatives or overlook certain vulnerabilities that require manual inspection.

9. Insufficient Follow-up and Verification:

After receiving a bug report, organizations should promptly verify the findings and maintain communication with researchers throughout the resolution process.

10. Failing to Address Ethical Concerns:

Some bug bounty programs may inadvertently incentivize unethical behavior or encourage researchers to engage in activities that could cause harm.

11. Ignoring Non-Technical Vulnerabilities:

Bug bounty programs should not overlook non-technical vulnerabilities, such as process flaws or policy violations, that could have a significant impact on security.

12. Disregarding the Human Element:

Organizations should recognize the importance of the human element in cybersecurity and consider factors like social engineering and user behavior in their bug bounty programs.

By learning from these failures, bug hunters and organizations can refine their bug bounty strategies and policies to create more effective and rewarding bug hunting experiences. Transparency, clear communication, and a commitment to continuous improvement are essential for building successful bug bounty programs and strengthening overall cybersecurity efforts.

8.4 Strategies for Overcoming Common Challenges

Bug hunting and participating in bug bounty programs can present various challenges for ethical hackers and security researchers. Successfully overcoming these challenges is key to becoming an effective bug hunter and contributing significantly to improving cybersecurity. Here are some strategies to overcome common challenges:

1. Scope Clarity:

Carefully review the bug bounty program's scope and guidelines before starting your bug hunting. Focus on areas explicitly allowed for testing to avoid wasting time on out-of-scope targets.

2. Effective Communication:

Establish clear and concise communication with program owners. Ask for clarifications if needed, and promptly respond to their inquiries during the bug hunting process.

3. Comprehensive Research:

Thoroughly research the technology, applications, and systems you are testing. Understand the latest attack vectors and common vulnerabilities related to the target technology.

4. Continuous Learning:

Stay updated on the latest cybersecurity trends, tools, and techniques. Participate in online communities, attend conferences, and read security research papers to enhance your knowledge.

5. Collaboration and Knowledge Sharing:

Engage with the bug hunting community and participate in knowledge-sharing forums. Collaborate with other researchers to learn from their experiences and share your insights.

6. Patience and Perseverance:

Bug hunting can be time-consuming and require patience. Stay persistent and remain dedicated to the process, even if you encounter initial setbacks.

7. Responsible Disclosure:

Always adhere to responsible disclosure practices. Avoid public disclosure before the organization has had a reasonable time to address the reported vulnerability.

8. Proper Vulnerability Reporting:

Write clear, detailed, and concise bug reports that include all necessary information for program owners to understand and reproduce the vulnerability.

9. Documentation and Record Keeping:

Keep detailed records of your bug hunting activities, including testing methodologies, findings, and communications with program owners. This documentation can be valuable for your future work.

10. Adaptability and Flexibility:

Be adaptable to changing circumstances, especially in bug bounty programs with evolving scopes and priorities.

11. Ethical and Professional Conduct:

Always adhere to ethical standards and maintain professional conduct during your bug hunting activities.

12. Seek Feedback and Learn from Failures:

If you encounter challenges or face failures, seek feedback from program owners or other experienced researchers. Use these experiences as learning opportunities to improve your bug hunting skills.

Overcoming challenges in bug hunting requires a combination of technical expertise, communication skills, and a dedication to ethical conduct. By continually refining your bug hunting strategies and learning from your experiences, you can become a more effective bug hunter and make valuable contributions to cybersecurity.

Chapter 9: Bug Bounty Hunting in IoT and OT Environments

In the ever-expanding realm of bug bounty hunting, the emergence of the Internet of Things (IoT) and Operational Technology (OT) brings forth new challenges and vulnerabilities to be conquered. Welcome to Chapter 9 of "Bug Bounty Unleashed: Mastering the Art of Ethical Hacking and Rewards." In this chapter, we explore the unique landscape of bug bounty hunting in IoT and OT environments, equipping you with the knowledge to secure these interconnected systems.

Understanding the IoT and OT Ecosystems

The IoT and OT ecosystems encompass a diverse array of interconnected devices and technologies, from smart homes to industrial control systems. We delve into the complexities of these environments, exploring the unique vulnerabilities and attack surfaces they present. By understanding the diverse landscape of IoT and OT, you will be prepared to navigate their security challenges effectively.

Identifying Vulnerabilities in IoT Devices

IoT devices, with their inherent interconnectivity, can become gateways for malicious attacks if not adequately secured. In this section, we discuss the vulnerabilities commonly found in IoT devices, including default credentials, lack of encryption, and weak authentication mechanisms. By mastering the art of uncovering IoT vulnerabilities, you will play a pivotal role in safeguarding the expanding world of IoT.

Securing OT Systems from Cyber Threats

Operational Technology (OT) systems, deployed in critical infrastructures like power plants and manufacturing facilities, demand robust security measures. We explore the vulnerabilities that OT systems face, such as legacy equipment, insecure communication protocols, and the potential for physical damage. By mastering the security of OT systems, you will protect essential infrastructures from potentially devastating cyber-physical attacks.

Exploring Connected Smart Environments

The integration of IoT technologies has given rise to interconnected smart environments, where homes, offices, and cities are interwoven through smart devices and systems. We examine the security implications of these connected environments, including the risks posed by smart home devices, building automation systems, and smart city infrastructure. By understanding these complexities, you will contribute to creating secure and resilient smart environments.

Confronting the Challenges of Firmware and Embedded Systems

Firmware and embedded systems form the backbone of IoT and OT devices, holding the potential for hidden vulnerabilities. We explore the intricacies of firmware security, including reverse engineering techniques and firmware analysis. By delving into the world of firmware and embedded systems, you will uncover vulnerabilities concealed deep within these devices.

Specialized Tools and Techniques for IoT and OT Bug Hunting

Bug hunting in IoT and OT environments demands specialized tools and techniques tailored to their unique challenges. We introduce you to tools and methodologies specifically designed for IoT and OT security assessments, equipping you with the means to conduct thorough and effective bug hunting in these domains.

Ethical Hacking in the Smart City Landscape

Smart cities represent a vision of the future, where technology enhances urban living. However, this vision comes with inherent security risks. We explore the security considerations of smart cities, including transportation systems, public utilities, and citizen services. By addressing the security of smart cities, you will shape the future of urban living while ensuring the safety and privacy of citizens.

In this chapter's conclusion, you will be equipped to embark on bug hunting expeditions in the dynamic landscapes of IoT and OT. As the boundaries of connected technologies expand, so does the need for skilled ethical hackers to secure these environments. Embrace the challenges of IoT and OT bug hunting with curiosity and determination, for your expertise will play a crucial role in shaping the secure future of interconnected systems.

9.1 Security Challenges in IoT Devices

IoT (Internet of Things) devices offer numerous benefits and conveniences, but they also introduce various security challenges that need to be addressed to ensure the safety and privacy of users. Some of the key security challenges in IoT devices include:

1. Weak Authentication and Authorization:

Many IoT devices use default or weak credentials, making them susceptible to brute-force attacks. Inadequate authorization mechanisms can also lead to unauthorized access to device functionalities.

2. Lack of Device Updates and Patch Management:

Manufacturers often neglect to provide timely updates and security patches for IoT devices. This leaves devices vulnerable to known vulnerabilities that could be exploited by attackers.

3. Insecure Communication Protocols:

IoT devices may use insecure communication protocols, such as unencrypted or poorly encrypted transmissions, making them susceptible to eavesdropping and man-in-the-middle attacks.

4. Vulnerable Firmware and Software:

Many IoT devices run on outdated or vulnerable firmware and software. Attackers can exploit these vulnerabilities to compromise the devices.

5. Physical Security and Tampering:

IoT devices deployed in uncontrolled or public environments may be physically tampered with or stolen, leading to security breaches and potential data exposure.

6. Lack of Device Identity and Authentication:

Without strong device identity and authentication mechanisms, it becomes challenging to ensure that only legitimate devices can communicate with authorized systems.

7. Data Privacy and Data Protection:

IoT devices often collect and process sensitive user data. Ensuring proper data privacy and protection becomes critical to prevent unauthorized access and data breaches.

8. Lack of Secure Boot and Trusted Execution Environment (TEE):

The absence of secure boot processes and TEEs can expose IoT devices to firmware tampering and unauthorized code execution.

9. Denial-of-Service (DoS) Attacks:

IoT devices can be targeted in DoS attacks, causing disruptions to their functionality or preventing legitimate users from accessing their services.

10. Lack of User Awareness and Control:

Many IoT devices are designed with limited user interfaces and controls, leading to users' inability to manage and secure their devices effectively.

11. Supply Chain Risks:

The complex supply chain involved in manufacturing IoT devices introduces potential security risks, such as compromised components or firmware.

12. Integration with Legacy Systems:

Integrating IoT devices with existing legacy systems can lead to security gaps if the older systems lack modern security measures.

Addressing these security challenges requires a multi-faceted approach involving manufacturers, developers, users, and policymakers. Implementing strong security measures, providing regular updates, and raising user awareness are essential steps to enhance the security posture of IoT devices and safeguard the growing IoT ecosystem.

9.2 Vulnerabilities in Operational Technology (OT)

Operational Technology (OT) refers to the hardware and software systems used to monitor, control, and manage physical processes in industries such as manufacturing, energy, transportation, and critical infrastructure. While OT systems play a crucial role in industrial processes, they are also susceptible to various vulnerabilities that can have significant real-world consequences. Some of the common vulnerabilities in OT systems include:

1. Outdated Software and Firmware:

Many OT systems use outdated software and firmware that may contain known vulnerabilities. Failure to update these components leaves systems exposed to exploitation.

2. Lack of Authentication and Authorization Mechanisms:

Weak or missing authentication and authorization mechanisms can allow unauthorized access to critical OT systems, leading to potential disruptions or sabotage.

3. Insecure Communication Protocols:

OT systems often use legacy communication protocols that lack encryption or strong authentication, making them susceptible to eavesdropping and man-in-the-middle attacks.

4. Default Credentials:

Some OT devices and systems come with default credentials that are not changed during installation. Attackers can exploit these defaults to gain unauthorized access.

5. Insufficient Physical Security:

Inadequate physical security measures can allow unauthorized personnel to access OT systems directly, potentially leading to unauthorized control or tampering.

6. Lack of Segmentation:

Failure to properly segment OT networks from other networks, such as IT networks, can increase the risk of lateral movement by attackers and compromise critical systems.

7. Vendor-Specific Vulnerabilities:

OT systems often use specialized hardware and software from various vendors. Vulnerabilities in vendor-specific components can be exploited to compromise the entire system.

8. Supply Chain Risks:

The supply chain for OT systems involves various vendors and third-party suppliers, creating opportunities for attackers to compromise components or introduce malicious software.

9. Lack of Incident Response Preparedness:

Many OT environments lack proper incident response plans and procedures, making it challenging to mitigate and recover from security incidents effectively.

10. Remote Access Vulnerabilities:

Remote access capabilities in OT systems, if not properly secured, can provide attackers with an entry point into critical infrastructure.

11. Inadequate Monitoring and Logging:

Insufficient monitoring and logging of OT system activities can hinder timely detection of security incidents and make it difficult to investigate and respond to threats.

12. Interoperability Issues:

Interoperability between different OT systems can create vulnerabilities, as misconfigurations or inconsistencies may arise during integration.

Given the critical nature of OT systems, addressing these vulnerabilities is of utmost importance. Organizations operating OT environments should implement comprehensive security measures, conduct regular assessments, and prioritize the protection of these systems to mitigate the risks posed by potential threats. Collaborative efforts between industry stakeholders, security researchers, and policymakers are essential to build a robust and secure OT ecosystem.

9.3 Hacking Smart Homes and Connected Devices

Hacking smart homes and connected devices poses significant security risks to homeowners and users. As more devices become part of the Internet of Things (IoT) ecosystem, the attack surface for cybercriminals expands, potentially leading to privacy breaches, property damage, and other serious consequences. Some common methods of hacking smart homes and connected devices include:

1. Default or Weak Credentials:

Many smart devices come with default credentials or weak passwords that users fail to change. Attackers can exploit these credentials to gain unauthorized access to the devices.

2. Vulnerable Firmware and Software:

Smart devices may have outdated or vulnerable firmware and software that cybercriminals can exploit to gain control over the devices.

3. Insecure Communication:

Smart devices may use unencrypted or poorly encrypted communication protocols, allowing attackers to intercept and manipulate data transmitted between devices and the cloud.

4. Man-in-the-Middle Attacks:

Cybercriminals can carry out man-in-the-middle attacks to intercept and modify data exchanged between smart devices and their associated apps or cloud services.

5. Exploiting Software Vulnerabilities:

Hackers may exploit software vulnerabilities in smart device apps or the cloud services to gain unauthorized access to users' devices or data.

6. Phishing and Social Engineering:

Cybercriminals may use phishing emails or social engineering techniques to trick users into revealing their login credentials or other sensitive information.

7. Brute-Force Attacks:

Attackers can attempt to gain unauthorized access to smart devices by using automated tools to try numerous combinations of usernames and passwords.

8. Lack of Security Updates:

Failure to update smart devices with the latest security patches leaves them vulnerable to known exploits.

9. Unauthorized Device Pairing:

Cybercriminals can try to pair their own devices with those of legitimate users, gaining control over the connected devices.

10. Physical Access:

If attackers gain physical access to a smart device, they may manipulate it directly or extract sensitive data from it.

11. Remote Code Execution:

Some smart devices may have vulnerabilities that allow remote code execution, enabling attackers to run malicious code on the device.

12. Home Network Vulnerabilities:

Weak Wi-Fi passwords, unsecured routers, and other vulnerabilities in the home network can expose smart devices to potential attacks.

To enhance the security of smart homes and connected devices, homeowners should take proactive steps, including:

- Changing default passwords to strong and unique ones for each device.
- Keeping smart device firmware and software up to date.
- Securing the home network with strong Wi-Fi passwords and encryption.
- Using two-factor authentication for device logins whenever possible.
- Avoiding suspicious links or emails and being cautious about granting device access to unknown apps or services.

By being vigilant and implementing proper security measures, users can minimize the risks of hacking and protect their smart homes and connected devices from potential cyber threats.

9.4 Safeguarding Industrial Control Systems (ICS)

Safeguarding Industrial Control Systems (ICS) is crucial to maintaining the safety, reliability, and integrity of critical infrastructure and industrial processes. As these systems are essential for controlling and monitoring various industrial operations, any compromise to their security could lead to severe consequences. Here are some key strategies for safeguarding Industrial Control Systems:

1. Network Segmentation:

Implement network segmentation to separate critical ICS networks from less critical networks, such as corporate IT networks and the internet. This reduces the attack surface and limits the potential impact of a security breach.

2. Strong Authentication and Access Controls:

Enforce strong authentication methods, such as multi-factor authentication (MFA), and implement access controls to limit system access only to authorized personnel.

3. Regular Security Assessments and Audits:

Conduct regular security assessments and audits of the ICS environment to identify vulnerabilities and weaknesses. Address any issues promptly and thoroughly.

4. Patch and Update Management:

Stay up to date with security patches and updates for all ICS components, including software, firmware, and operating systems, to prevent exploitation of known vulnerabilities.

5. Secure Communication Protocols:

Use secure communication protocols, such as encryption and VPNs, to protect data transmitted between ICS components.

6. Monitoring and Intrusion Detection:

Deploy robust monitoring and intrusion detection systems to detect and respond to any anomalous activities or potential security breaches in real-time.

7. Incident Response and Recovery Plan:

Develop and regularly test an incident response and recovery plan to ensure that personnel are prepared to handle and mitigate security incidents effectively.

8. Physical Security Measures:

Implement physical security measures to prevent unauthorized access to critical ICS components and control rooms.

9. Training and Awareness:

Provide comprehensive cybersecurity training and awareness programs for all personnel involved in operating and maintaining the ICS environment. Educate employees about common security risks, such as phishing attacks.

10. Vendor Management and Supply Chain Security:

Assess the security practices of ICS vendors and third-party suppliers. Establish clear security requirements for vendors and ensure they follow secure coding practices.

11. Regular Backups:

Regularly back up critical ICS data and configurations to enable efficient recovery in case of a security incident or system failure.

12. Compliance with Industry Standards and Regulations:

Ensure compliance with relevant industry standards and regulations, such as NIST SP 800-82, IEC 62443, and others that provide guidelines for securing ICS environments.

By adopting these strategies, organizations can enhance the security posture of their Industrial Control Systems and mitigate the risk of cyber threats. Safeguarding ICS is a continuous effort that requires collaboration among various stakeholders, including IT and OT personnel, executives, and security experts, to ensure the resilience and reliability of critical infrastructure and industrial processes.

Chapter 10: Bug Bounty Hunting in Cloud and Containerized Environments

In the age of cloud computing and containerization, bug bounty hunters must adapt their skills to secure these dynamic and rapidly evolving environments. Welcome to Chapter 10 of "Bug Bounty Unleashed: Mastering the Art of Ethical Hacking and Rewards." In this chapter, we explore the complexities of bug bounty hunting in cloud and containerized environments, equipping you with the knowledge to navigate these cutting-edge technologies.

Understanding Cloud Computing and Virtualization

Cloud computing has transformed the way organizations deploy and manage their infrastructure. We explore the fundamentals of cloud computing, including Infrastructure as a Service (IaaS), Platform as a Service (PaaS), and Software as a Service (SaaS). Additionally, we delve into virtualization technologies that underpin cloud environments, such as hypervisors and virtual machines. By understanding these technologies, you will be better prepared to uncover vulnerabilities within cloud-based systems.

Identifying Security Risks in Cloud Services

Cloud services offer immense flexibility and scalability, but they also introduce new security risks. We discuss the common security challenges faced by cloud services, such as misconfigurations, data breaches, and shared responsibility models. By honing your ability to identify cloud-specific vulnerabilities, you will contribute to fortifying the security posture of cloud-based applications and services.

Securing Serverless Architectures

Serverless architectures have gained popularity for their efficiency and cost-effectiveness. However, the security implications of serverless computing require careful consideration. We explore the security risks associated with serverless architectures, including privilege escalation, injection attacks, and event data injection. By mastering serverless security, you will ensure the integrity and resilience of serverless applications.

Containerization and Docker Security

Containerization has revolutionized software development and deployment. We delve into the security considerations of containerization technologies like Docker, examining the risks associated with insecure container configurations, container escape vulnerabilities, and containerized application security. By securing containerized environments, you will play a pivotal role in protecting the future of agile and scalable application deployment.

Exploiting Kubernetes Vulnerabilities

Kubernetes has emerged as a leading platform for container orchestration. However, misconfigurations and vulnerabilities in Kubernetes deployments can expose organizations to significant risks. We explore common Kubernetes security issues, such as privilege escalation, insecure API configurations, and lateral movement within clusters. By mastering Kubernetes security, you will contribute to the robustness of containerized infrastructure.

The Role of DevOps in Bug Bounty Hunting

The integration of DevOps practices has accelerated the pace of software development and deployment. We discuss the intersection of DevOps and bug bounty hunting, emphasizing the importance of collaboration and communication between developers and bug hunters. By aligning with DevOps principles, you will seamlessly integrate security into the software development lifecycle.

Automating Cloud and Containerized Bug Hunting

The dynamic nature of cloud and containerized environments demands efficient bug hunting strategies. We explore automation tools and techniques specific to cloud and container security assessments. By automating repetitive tasks and vulnerability scanning, you will optimize your bug hunting efforts and uncover vulnerabilities with greater speed and accuracy.

In this chapter's conclusion, you will be equipped with the expertise to navigate cloud and containerized environments with confidence and skill. As organizations increasingly embrace cloud computing and containerization, your contributions as an ethical hacker will become instrumental in safeguarding the integrity and security of these innovative technologies.

10.1 Securing Cloud Services and Infrastructure

Securing cloud services and infrastructure is essential for organizations that rely on cloud computing to store and process their data, applications, and services. Cloud security measures are crucial to protect sensitive information, maintain data privacy, and ensure the availability and integrity of cloud resources. Here are some key strategies to secure cloud services and infrastructure:

1. Strong Identity and Access Management (IAM):

Implement robust IAM practices, including strong authentication, multi-factor authentication (MFA), and least privilege access controls to ensure that only authorized users have access to cloud resources.

2. Data Encryption:

Encrypt data both in transit and at rest to safeguard it from unauthorized access and maintain data confidentiality.

3. Secure APIs and Interfaces:

Securely design and configure APIs and interfaces to prevent unauthorized access and potential API-related attacks, such as injection attacks.

4. Regular Security Assessments and Penetration Testing:

Conduct regular security assessments and penetration testing of cloud infrastructure and applications to identify and remediate vulnerabilities proactively.

5. Security Monitoring and Logging:

Deploy continuous security monitoring and logging to detect and respond to security incidents in real-time.

6. Compliance and Governance:

Adhere to industry-specific compliance requirements and best practices while defining cloud governance policies to ensure security and data privacy.

7. Patch Management:

Regularly update and patch cloud infrastructure components to protect against known vulnerabilities.

8. Network Security:

Employ network security controls, such as firewalls, intrusion detection and prevention systems (IDPS), and virtual private clouds (VPCs), to secure cloud networks.

9. Secure Configuration Management:

Follow secure configuration practices for cloud resources, services, and virtual machines to minimize the attack surface.

10. Disaster Recovery and Business Continuity Planning:

Implement robust disaster recovery and business continuity plans to ensure data availability and seamless operations in case of disruptions.

11. Vendor and Third-Party Security Evaluation:

Assess the security practices of cloud service providers and third-party vendors to ensure they meet your organization's security standards.

12. Employee Training and Awareness:

Educate employees about cloud security best practices, such as recognizing phishing attempts and following secure data handling procedures.

Adopting a defense-in-depth approach, where multiple layers of security controls are implemented, is crucial for securing cloud services and infrastructure effectively. Additionally, regular security updates, monitoring, and ongoing security awareness training are essential to maintain a robust cloud security posture. Organizations should also stay informed about the latest cloud security threats and best practices to stay ahead of emerging risks and vulnerabilities.

10.2 Exploring Container Security Issues

Containerization has revolutionized software development and deployment by providing a lightweight and scalable solution for packaging applications and their dependencies. However, like any technology, containers also come with their security challenges. Here are some common container security issues:

1. Vulnerable Images:

Using container images with outdated or vulnerable software components can expose containers to known exploits and security breaches.

2. Image Integrity and Authenticity:

Ensuring the integrity and authenticity of container images is crucial to prevent the deployment of tampered or malicious images.

3. Privilege Escalation:

Containers running with excessive privileges can be exploited by attackers to gain unauthorized access to the host system or other containers.

4. Container Breakouts:

Inadequately secured containers may be susceptible to container escape attacks, where an attacker gains unauthorized access to the underlying host system.

5. Insecure Configuration:

Misconfigurations in container settings can lead to security vulnerabilities, such as unnecessary access to host resources or network exposure.

6. Shared Kernel Vulnerabilities:

Containers on the same host share the host's kernel. If a vulnerability is exploited in the kernel, it could impact all containers on that host.

7. Resource Exhaustion Attacks:

Attackers may exploit poorly configured containers to perform resource exhaustion attacks, causing denial of service to legitimate users.

8. Inadequate Isolation:

Insecurely isolated containers may enable unauthorized access to sensitive data or resources shared between containers.

9. Container Registry Security:

Insecurely managed container registries can lead to unauthorized access to images or potentially expose sensitive information.

10. Lack of Runtime Monitoring:

- Failure to monitor container runtime behavior can make it difficult to detect suspicious activities or security incidents.

11. Container Sprawl:

- Rapid container deployment without proper management can lead to "container sprawl," making it harder to track and secure all instances.

12. Orphaned Containers and Images:

- Orphaned containers or unused images can be forgotten and left unpatched, introducing security risks.

To address these container security issues, organizations can adopt several best practices:

- Use only trusted and signed container images from reputable sources.
- Regularly update container images and apply security patches.
- Implement least privilege principles for container configurations.
- Use container security tools for vulnerability scanning and image integrity verification.
- Employ security measures like container network policies, namespaces, and seccomp profiles for improved isolation.

- Implement runtime security monitoring and log analysis for containers.

By implementing these practices and continuously improving container security, organizations can harness the benefits of containerization while mitigating potential risks and threats.

10.3 Hunting Vulnerabilities in Serverless Architectures

Hunting vulnerabilities in serverless architectures requires a different approach compared to traditional monolithic or virtualized setups. Serverless computing, often based on Function as a Service (FaaS), introduces unique security challenges due to its event-driven nature and reliance on third-party cloud providers. Here are some key aspects to consider when hunting for vulnerabilities in serverless architectures:

1. Event Injection and Data Validation:

Check for potential event injection vulnerabilities, where untrusted data is used to trigger serverless functions. Validate and sanitize inputs to prevent injection attacks.

2. Insecure Serverless Code:

Review serverless function code for security flaws, such as SQL injection, command injection, or insecure deserialization.

3. Inadequate Permissions and Access Control:

Ensure that serverless functions have the appropriate permissions and access controls to prevent unauthorized access to resources.

4. Resource Exhaustion and Denial of Service (DoS):

Identify potential resource exhaustion vulnerabilities in serverless functions that attackers could exploit to cause DoS.

5. Cold Start Attacks:

Investigate possible security implications during the cold start of serverless functions, where delays could lead to increased exposure to certain attacks.

6. Serverless-Specific Vulnerabilities:

Familiarize yourself with serverless-specific vulnerabilities, such as the "event data injection" vulnerability, which affects AWS Lambda functions.

7. Dependencies and Vulnerable Libraries:

Audit third-party dependencies and libraries used in serverless functions for known vulnerabilities.

8. Data Storage and Encryption:

Ensure that sensitive data is properly encrypted when stored and transmitted within serverless functions.

9. Logging and Monitoring:

Implement robust logging and monitoring to detect any anomalous behavior or security incidents within serverless functions.

10. Isolation and Multi-Tenancy:

- Check for potential security issues related to the shared execution environment in serverless platforms.

11. Cloud Provider Security Configuration:

- Verify that your cloud provider's security configurations are properly set to protect serverless functions and their associated resources.

12. Secure Coding Practices:

- Encourage secure coding practices among developers creating serverless functions and offer appropriate training and guidance.

Furthermore, leveraging serverless security tools and frameworks, such as AWS Lambda Runtime Interface Client (RIC), AWS Lambda Extensions, or Azure Functions Security Center, can aid in identifying and addressing potential vulnerabilities. Regular security assessments, code reviews, and penetration testing specific to serverless architectures are also essential components of a comprehensive vulnerability hunting strategy in this context.

It is essential to stay updated with the latest security best practices and developments in serverless security to effectively hunt for vulnerabilities and maintain a secure serverless environment.

10.4 DevSecOps and Integrating Security in CI/CD Pipelines

DevSecOps is an approach that emphasizes the integration of security practices into the DevOps (Development and Operations) workflow. By embedding security into every stage of the CI/CD (Continuous Integration/Continuous Deployment) pipeline, organizations can identify and address security issues early in the software development lifecycle. Here are some key steps to integrate security into CI/CD pipelines effectively:

1. Security Requirements and Policies:

Define clear security requirements and policies that align with the organization's risk appetite and compliance needs. These requirements will guide the security practices throughout the pipeline.

2. Security Training and Awareness:

Ensure that all members of the development and operations teams receive security training and are aware of security best practices.

3. Security Code Reviews and Static Analysis:

Integrate security code reviews and static code analysis tools into the CI/CD pipeline to identify and fix security vulnerabilities in the code early in the development process.

4. Security Testing:

Automate security testing processes, such as dynamic application security testing (DAST) and software composition analysis (SCA), to identify vulnerabilities and insecure dependencies.

5. Secure Configuration Management:

Use infrastructure as code (IaC) and configuration management tools to ensure that cloud resources and infrastructure are configured securely.

6. Container Security Scanning:

Implement container security scanning to identify vulnerabilities in container images used in the CI/CD pipeline.

7. Secrets Management:

Use a secure secrets management system to manage sensitive information, such as API keys and passwords, in the CI/CD process.

8. Access Control and Least Privilege:

Apply the principle of least privilege to limit access to CI/CD tools and resources, reducing the risk of unauthorized access.

9. Continuous Compliance Monitoring:

Implement continuous compliance monitoring to ensure that the CI/CD pipeline and associated resources remain compliant with security standards and regulations.

10. Automated Security Gates:

- Set up automated security gates in the pipeline that check for security requirements before allowing code to progress to the next stage.

11. Incident Response Plan:

- Develop and regularly test an incident response plan specific to security incidents that may occur in the CI/CD pipeline.

12. Collaboration and Communication:

- Foster collaboration between development, operations, and security teams to facilitate the sharing of security insights and the collective ownership of security responsibilities.

By integrating security into the CI/CD pipeline, organizations can identify and address security issues earlier, reducing the cost and effort associated with fixing vulnerabilities in later stages of development. Continuous security checks and automation help ensure that security is not seen as an impediment but as an integral part of the software development process, promoting a culture of secure coding and deployment.

Chapter 11: Maximizing Bug Bounty Rewards and Recognition

In the world of bug bounty hunting, the pursuit of valuable rewards and recognition for your contributions is a natural aspiration. Welcome to Chapter 11 of "Bug Bounty Unleashed: Mastering the Art of Ethical Hacking and Rewards." In this chapter, we explore strategies and insights to maximize your bug bounty rewards and gain recognition as a skilled and respected bug hunter.

Honing Your Bug Hunting Skills

The foundation of maximizing bug bounty rewards begins with honing your bug hunting skills. We discuss the importance of continuous learning and staying up-to-date with the latest security trends and vulnerabilities. By improving your technical prowess and problem-solving abilities, you will increase your chances of discovering high-impact bugs.

Choosing the Right Bug Bounty Programs

Not all bug bounty programs are created equal. We explore strategies for selecting the right bug bounty programs based on your expertise and interests. By focusing on programs that align with your skills, you will optimize your efforts and increase your likelihood of successful bug submissions.

Strategizing Your Bug Hunting Efforts

Effective bug hunting requires strategic planning and execution. We delve into various bug hunting strategies, including focusing on specific vulnerability types, analyzing the attack surface, and leveraging automation. By strategizing your bug hunting efforts, you will work smarter, not harder, and achieve more impactful results.

Effective Communication with Program Owners

Effective communication with program owners is crucial for maximizing rewards and gaining recognition. We explore strategies for articulating the impact of discovered vulnerabilities and the value they bring to the organization. By building rapport and fostering open dialogue, you will strengthen your relationship with program owners and enhance the rewards you receive.

Bug Bounty Incentive Programs and Swag

Bug bounty programs often offer additional incentives and rewards beyond monetary payouts. We discuss incentive programs, bonuses, and bug bounty swag, showcasing how these rewards can motivate and incentivize bug hunters. By leveraging these additional perks, you will not only maximize your rewards but also enjoy the recognition of your contributions.

Contributing to the Bug Bounty Community

Active participation in the bug bounty community is a powerful means of gaining recognition and respect. We explore the benefits of sharing knowledge, collaborating with fellow hunters, and engaging with program owners. By contributing to the community, you will establish yourself as a trusted and valuable member of the bug bounty ecosystem.

Building a Strong Bug Bounty Portfolio

A strong bug bounty portfolio serves as a testament to your expertise and accomplishments. We discuss strategies for organizing and showcasing your bug reports, demonstrating your impact in a clear and compelling manner. By maintaining a well-documented portfolio, you will enhance your credibility and attract more opportunities for bug hunting.

In this chapter's conclusion, you will possess a comprehensive toolkit for maximizing bug bounty rewards and gaining recognition in the bug hunting community. By honing your skills, selecting the right programs, and strategizing your efforts, you will embark on a rewarding journey filled with opportunities for growth and professional acclaim.

11.1 Negotiation Strategies for Bug Bounties

Negotiation strategies play a vital role in bug bounty programs, as they can determine the final rewards for discovered vulnerabilities and the overall success of the collaboration between the bug hunter and the organization running the program. Here are some effective negotiation strategies for bug bounties:

1. Understand the Program Rules and Scope:

Before starting the negotiation, thoroughly read and understand the bug bounty program's rules, scope, and reward guidelines. Make sure your findings fall within the program's defined criteria.

2. Provide Clear and Detailed Reports:

Present clear and well-structured reports detailing the discovered vulnerabilities, their impact, and possible exploitation scenarios. This helps the organization better understand the severity of the issues and may lead to higher rewards.

3. Know the Market Value:

Be aware of the market value for similar vulnerabilities and the typical reward amounts offered in other bug bounty programs. This knowledge can guide your negotiation strategy and help you justify your reward expectations.

4. Be Respectful and Professional:

Approach the negotiation process with professionalism and respect. Avoid being confrontational or demanding, as it may create a negative impression and affect the outcome.

5. Be Flexible:

Be open to negotiation and consider the organization's perspective on the severity and impact of the reported vulnerabilities. Be willing to adjust your expectations if the organization provides valid reasons for a lower reward.

6. Prioritize Critical Vulnerabilities:

If your findings include critical vulnerabilities with high potential impact, highlight their severity during the negotiation. Critical vulnerabilities are more likely to warrant higher rewards.

7. Communicate Clearly:

Clearly articulate your findings, the efforts you invested, and the potential risks associated with the vulnerabilities. Provide any necessary proof of concept to demonstrate the impact of the reported issues.

8. Build a Good Relationship:

Establish a positive and professional relationship with the organization's security team. Building trust and rapport may lead to more fruitful negotiations and future opportunities.

9. Respect Program Deadlines:

Adhere to the program's disclosure timeline and avoid public disclosure of vulnerabilities until the organization has had sufficient time to address them. Premature disclosure may negatively impact the negotiation process.

10. Consider Non-Monetary Rewards:

- In some cases, organizations may offer non-monetary rewards, such as public recognition or swag. Consider these rewards as part of the negotiation process, especially if they align with your interests.

11. Evaluate Counter Offers Carefully:

- If the organization makes a counteroffer, evaluate it thoroughly and consider whether it aligns with your effort and the severity of the vulnerabilities discovered.

12. Maintain Professionalism throughout the Process:

- Regardless of the outcome, maintain a professional attitude throughout the negotiation process. A positive experience may lead to future collaborations and increased trust between you and the organization.

Remember that negotiation is a collaborative process, and both bug hunters and organizations seek to benefit from the bug bounty program. By employing these strategies and maintaining professionalism, you can increase the likelihood of reaching a fair and satisfactory agreement for both parties involved.

11.2 Building a Reputation in the Bug Bounty Community

Building a reputation in the bug bounty community is essential for bug hunters who want to be recognized for their skills, expertise, and contributions to cybersecurity. A positive reputation can open up new opportunities, increase visibility, and lead to more lucrative bug bounty engagements. Here are some strategies to build a strong reputation in the bug bounty community:

1. Consistent Ethical Behavior:

Always adhere to ethical hacking principles and responsible disclosure practices. Avoid any activities that could harm organizations or violate bug bounty program rules.

2. Quality Bug Reports:

Submit high-quality and well-documented bug reports that are clear, detailed, and reproducible. Well-structured reports demonstrate professionalism and contribute to faster issue resolution.

3. Active Participation:

Actively engage in bug bounty programs and security research projects. Regularly participate in bug hunting challenges and publicize your findings responsibly.

4. Vulnerability Disclosure:

Follow responsible disclosure practices when reporting vulnerabilities. Coordinate with program owners to ensure vulnerabilities are fixed before public disclosure.

5. Continuous Learning:

Stay updated on the latest cybersecurity trends, tools, and techniques. Participate in training courses, workshops, and conferences to enhance your knowledge and skills.

6. Collaboration and Knowledge Sharing:

Engage with the bug bounty community through forums, social media, and security conferences. Share your experiences, insights, and knowledge to contribute to the community's growth.

7. Be Approachable and Helpful:

Be approachable and willing to assist fellow bug hunters. Answer questions, provide guidance, and share tips to help others succeed.

8. Public Write-ups and Contributions:

Publish public write-ups of your successful bug bounty findings, demonstrating your skills and problem-solving abilities. Contribute to security blogs or open-source projects to showcase your expertise.

9. Recognition and Acknowledgment:

Request and showcase acknowledgment for your contributions in bug bounty program hall of fames or security researcher lists.

10. Positive Interactions with Program Owners:

- Maintain professional and positive interactions with program owners and security teams. Build a reputation as a reliable and responsible researcher.

11. Specialize and Demonstrate Expertise:

- Consider specializing in specific technologies, platforms, or types of vulnerabilities. Demonstrating expertise in a particular area can make you more sought after by organizations.

12. Patience and Perseverance:

- Building a reputation takes time and effort. Be patient and persistent in your bug hunting journey. Consistent contributions and dedication will eventually be recognized.

Remember that building a reputation in the bug bounty community is an ongoing process. Demonstrate professionalism, ethical conduct, and a commitment to learning and improving your skills. By actively participating in the community, sharing knowledge, and contributing responsibly, you can establish yourself as a respected and valuable member of the bug bounty community.

11.3 Leveraging Bug Bounty Platforms for Recognition

Leveraging bug bounty platforms is an effective way for bug hunters to gain recognition for their skills and contributions to cybersecurity. These platforms provide a structured and organized environment for security researchers to discover vulnerabilities, report them to organizations, and potentially earn rewards. Here are some strategies to leverage bug bounty platforms for recognition:

1. Active Participation:

Actively participate in bug bounty programs on various platforms. Regularly scan for new programs and challenges to maximize your opportunities for finding vulnerabilities.

2. Consistent Bug Hunting:

Consistently hunt for bugs and report them responsibly. Regularly submitting valuable bug reports can increase your visibility and reputation on the platform.

3. High-Quality Reports:

Focus on submitting high-quality bug reports that are clear, detailed, and easy to reproduce. A well-structured report demonstrates professionalism and increases the chances of your findings being recognized.

4. Public Bug Bounty Profiles:

Most bug bounty platforms allow researchers to create public profiles showcasing their achievements and contributions. Ensure that your profile is up-to-date and highlights your successful submissions.

5. Write-ups and Case Studies:

Write detailed and informative public write-ups of your successful bug reports. Share them on the bug bounty platform and other cybersecurity communities to gain recognition for your expertise.

6. Contribution to the Community:

Engage with the bug bounty community on the platform. Share your experiences, insights, and knowledge in forums or discussion boards. Help other researchers and contribute to the community's growth.

7. Recognition and Rewards:

Seek acknowledgment from organizations for your findings. Public recognition in hall of fames, researcher acknowledgments, or leaderboards enhances your reputation on the platform.

8. Specialization and Expertise:

Consider specializing in specific domains, technologies, or types of vulnerabilities. Demonstrating expertise in a particular area can make you stand out and attract attention from organizations seeking specialized researchers.

9. Collaboration with Program Owners:

Maintain positive and professional interactions with program owners and security teams. Building a reputation as a reliable and responsible researcher can lead to repeat engagements.

10. Networking and Collaboration:

- Network with other bug hunters and security professionals on the platform. Collaborating with others on challenging bug hunting projects can showcase your teamwork and problem-solving abilities.

11. Platform Bug Hunter Ranks:

- Some bug bounty platforms have ranking systems based on researchers' contributions and performance.

Strive to improve your rank, as higher ranks often gain more visibility and recognition.

12. Continuous Learning and Improvement:

- Stay updated on the latest security trends, tools, and techniques. Continuously improve your skills to remain competitive and relevant in the bug bounty community.

Remember that recognition on bug bounty platforms is earned over time through consistent efforts and valuable contributions. Be patient, persevere, and maintain a positive and ethical approach to your bug hunting journey. The more you actively engage with the community and demonstrate your expertise, the more recognition and opportunities you are likely to receive.

11.4 Bug Bounty Hall of Fame and Acknowledgments

Bug bounty Hall of Fame and acknowledgments are important ways for organizations to recognize and appreciate the contributions of security researchers who have responsibly reported vulnerabilities in their systems. These public acknowledgments serve as a form of recognition and provide bug hunters with a platform to showcase their achievements and expertise. Here's how bug bounty Hall of Fame and acknowledgments work:

1. Bug Bounty Hall of Fame:

Bug bounty Hall of Fame is a dedicated page or section on the organization's website or security portal. It lists the names or pseudonyms of security researchers who have reported valid security vulnerabilities in the organization's systems.

2. Acknowledgment Criteria:

Organizations typically have criteria for acknowledging researchers in their Hall of Fame. This could include the severity and impact of the reported vulnerabilities, the quality of the bug report, and adherence to responsible disclosure practices.

3. Public Recognition:

Researchers' names or aliases are publicly displayed on the Hall of Fame page, giving them recognition for their valuable contributions to the organization's security.

4. Profile and Achievement Showcase:

For security researchers, having their name listed on an organization's Hall of Fame acts as a testament to their skills and accomplishments. Researchers often link to their Hall of Fame profiles on their public bug bounty profiles or resumes.

5. Gratitude and Incentive:

Acknowledging security researchers in the Hall of Fame is a way for organizations to show their gratitude for the researchers' efforts in helping improve their security posture. This, in turn, may incentivize more researchers to participate in their bug bounty programs.

6. Positive Relationship Building:

Recognizing security researchers publicly fosters a positive relationship between the organization and the bug hunting community. It encourages researchers to continue reporting vulnerabilities and fosters a collaborative environment.

7. Transparency and Trust:

Bug bounty Hall of Fame promotes transparency by publicly acknowledging the efforts of researchers and demonstrating the organization's commitment to security.

8. Acknowledgments in Reports:

Some organizations also include researcher acknowledgments in their security advisories or vulnerability disclosure reports, further highlighting the contributions of the researchers.

9. Ranking and Leaderboards:

Some bug bounty platforms offer ranking and leaderboards based on researchers' performance. Achieving higher rankings can lead to more visibility and recognition within the bug hunting community.

10. Swag and Rewards:

- In addition to Hall of Fame recognition, some organizations may offer swag, special rewards, or bonuses to researchers who have made significant contributions or achieved exceptional results.

Bug bounty Hall of Fame and acknowledgments are powerful motivators for researchers and play a crucial role in building a strong bug hunting community. They serve as a win-win for both organizations and security researchers, creating a collaborative and mutually beneficial relationship in the realm of cybersecurity.

Chapter 12: The Future of Bug Bounty Hunting

As bug bounty hunting continues to evolve, the future holds exciting prospects for ethical hackers and organizations alike. Welcome to Chapter 12 of "Bug Bounty Unleashed: Mastering the Art of Ethical Hacking and Rewards." In this final chapter, we explore the promising future of bug bounty hunting and the transformative impact it will have on the cybersecurity landscape.

Expanding Attack Surfaces in Emerging Technologies

The proliferation of emerging technologies, such as 5G, Internet of Things (IoT), and Artificial Intelligence (AI), will create new attack surfaces for ethical hackers to explore. We discuss the potential vulnerabilities that may arise in these technologies and the corresponding opportunities for skilled bug hunters to secure them.

Incorporating AI and Automation in Bug Hunting

The integration of AI and automation will revolutionize bug hunting, streamlining vulnerability discovery and response. We explore the potential applications of AI in vulnerability scanning, pattern recognition, and behavior analysis. By leveraging AI-driven automation, bug hunters will be equipped to scale their efforts and uncover vulnerabilities with unparalleled efficiency.

Blockchain Security Challenges and Opportunities

Blockchain technology introduces unique security challenges, as well as opportunities for ethical hackers to uncover vulnerabilities in decentralized systems. We explore the complexities of blockchain security, including smart contract vulnerabilities and consensus protocol weaknesses. By addressing these challenges, bug hunters will play a vital role in fortifying blockchain-based applications and systems.

Bug Bounty Programs in Non-Traditional Sectors

As the scope of bug bounty programs broadens, non-traditional sectors such as healthcare, automotive, and aerospace will recognize the value of bug hunting. We discuss the potential for bug bounty programs in these sectors to improve the security of critical systems and protect user data.

Government and Global Collaboration in Bug Bounties

The involvement of governments and international organizations in bug bounties will foster global collaboration for a safer cyber landscape. We explore the implications of government-led bug bounty initiatives and the potential for collective efforts to combat cyber threats.

The Evolution of Responsible Disclosure Policies

Responsible disclosure policies will continue to evolve, adapting to the ever-changing cybersecurity landscape. We discuss the potential for more standardized disclosure guidelines and increased cooperation between ethical hackers and organizations in the responsible disclosure process.

Addressing Ethical Challenges and Privacy Concerns

As bug bounty hunting progresses, ethical challenges and privacy concerns will demand increased attention. We explore the ethical considerations of bug hunting in sensitive sectors and the importance of privacy protection in the bug hunting process.

Empowering the Next Generation of Bug Hunters

The future of bug bounty hunting rests in the hands of the next generation of ethical hackers. We discuss the significance of educational initiatives and mentorship programs to empower aspiring bug hunters and foster a diverse and inclusive bug hunting community.

In this chapter's conclusion, we envision a future where bug bounty hunting plays a pivotal role in securing emerging technologies and safeguarding critical systems. By embracing advancements in AI, blockchain, and automation, ethical hackers will thrive in a dynamic and ever-changing cybersecurity landscape.

As you embark on your bug bounty hunting journey, remember that the future is not just about discovering vulnerabilities; it is about making a positive impact on the security of the digital world. Embrace the challenges, seize the opportunities, and continue mastering the art of ethical hacking for a safer and more secure cyber future.

12.1 Emerging Trends in Ethical Hacking

As the field of cybersecurity constantly evolves, ethical hacking also experiences emerging trends and developments. These trends reflect the changing landscape of threats, technologies, and security practices. Here are some emerging trends in ethical hacking:

1. IoT and OT Security Challenges:

With the increasing adoption of Internet of Things (IoT) and Operational Technology (OT) devices, ethical hackers are focusing on identifying vulnerabilities in these connected systems. Securing critical infrastructure, smart homes, and industrial control systems are becoming essential areas of focus.

2. Cloud Security Assessments:

As cloud computing continues to be the backbone of modern IT infrastructures, ethical hackers are paying more attention to identifying cloud-related vulnerabilities and misconfigurations.

3. Container and Microservices Security:

Containers and microservices architecture are gaining popularity for their scalability and agility. Ethical hackers are now exploring the unique security challenges posed by these technologies, such as container escape attacks and insecure configurations.

4. AI and ML in Cybersecurity:

Artificial Intelligence (AI) and Machine Learning (ML) are being integrated into cybersecurity tools and solutions. Ethical hackers are exploring potential vulnerabilities in AI/ML algorithms and applications, including evasion techniques against AI-based security controls.

5. Red Team Operations and Adversarial Simulation:

Organizations are increasingly conducting red team operations and adversarial simulations to assess their security posture. Ethical hackers simulate real-world attacks to identify gaps in defense and response capabilities.

6. Bug Bounty and Vulnerability Coordination Programs:

Bug bounty and vulnerability coordination programs are becoming more prevalent among organizations as a proactive approach to identifying and resolving security issues. Ethical hackers play a vital role in such programs.

7. Mobile and App Security:

With the proliferation of mobile devices and applications, ethical hackers are focusing on finding vulnerabilities in mobile apps and related infrastructure.

8. Biometric and Authentication Security:

Ethical hackers are testing the security of biometric authentication systems, exploring potential flaws and challenges in biometric data protection.

9. Blockchain Security:

As blockchain technology gains traction, ethical hackers are scrutinizing blockchain implementations and smart contracts for potential vulnerabilities.

10. Quantum Computing and Post-Quantum Cryptography:

- Ethical hackers are researching the security implications of quantum computing and exploring post-quantum cryptographic solutions to protect against quantum threats.

11. Securing AI-based Systems:

- Ethical hackers are assessing AI-based systems for security risks, including the potential for adversarial attacks and bias in AI decision-making.

12. Supply Chain Security:

- Ethical hackers are evaluating supply chain security, including software supply chain attacks, to assess the risks of third-party dependencies.

Ethical hacking is a dynamic field, and these emerging trends highlight the need for continuous learning and adaptation. Ethical hackers must stay informed about the latest technologies, attack vectors, and security practices to effectively protect organizations from ever-evolving cyber threats.

12.2 Challenges and Opportunities in Bug Bounties

Bug bounties offer both challenges and opportunities for organizations and security researchers. Understanding these aspects is essential for successful bug bounty programs and maximizing the benefits they can provide. Here are some of the key challenges and opportunities in bug bounties:

Challenges:

1. Scope and Coverage:

Defining the scope of a bug bounty program can be challenging. Organizations must carefully outline what systems are in scope and what types of vulnerabilities are eligible for rewards.

2. False Positives and Duplicate Reports:

Bug bounty programs often receive duplicate reports or submissions that don't qualify as valid vulnerabilities. Sorting through these false positives can consume time and resources.

3. Vulnerability Severity Assessment:

Determining the severity and impact of reported vulnerabilities accurately can be difficult, as it requires understanding the potential consequences of each flaw.

4. Communication and Coordination:

Effective communication and coordination between bug hunters and program owners are crucial for resolving issues promptly and avoiding misunderstandings.

5. Resource Management:

Organizations must allocate resources to handle incoming reports, verify vulnerabilities, and provide timely responses and rewards.

6. Legal and Compliance Considerations:

Bug bounty programs must adhere to legal requirements and ensure that researchers' actions comply with applicable laws and regulations.

7. Reporting Quality:

Some bug reports may lack essential details or be poorly structured, making it challenging for program owners to understand the issue fully.

Opportunities:

1. Early Vulnerability Detection:

Bug bounties enable organizations to identify and remediate security vulnerabilities before malicious actors can exploit them.

2. Diverse Skill Sets:

Bug bounty programs attract a diverse pool of security researchers, each with unique skills and expertise, increasing the likelihood of discovering different types of vulnerabilities.

3. Cost-Effective Security Testing:

Bug bounties can be more cost-effective than traditional penetration testing, as organizations only pay for valid results.

4. Positive Public Image:

Running a successful bug bounty program can enhance an organization's reputation as security-conscious and committed to protecting user data.

5. Continuous Security Testing:

Bug bounty programs allow organizations to maintain continuous security testing and response to evolving threats.

6. Community Collaboration:

Bug bounties foster collaboration and communication between organizations and the broader security research community.

7. Identifying New Attack Vectors:

Bug bounties can help organizations discover new and innovative attack vectors that may not have been previously considered.

8. Talent Recruitment and Retention:

Successful bug bounty programs can attract top security talent to the organization and encourage ongoing collaboration.

To make the most of bug bounties, organizations should be prepared to address these challenges and capitalize on the opportunities they present. By maintaining clear communication, providing prompt and fair rewards, and continually improving their security practices based on bug bounty findings, organizations can build successful bug bounty programs that benefit both their cybersecurity posture and the wider security community.

12.3 The Rise of AI in Bug Bounty Hunting

The rise of Artificial Intelligence (AI) in bug bounty hunting is transforming the way security researchers identify vulnerabilities and contribute to cybersecurity. AI is being leveraged in various aspects of bug bounty hunting to enhance efficiency, accuracy, and overall effectiveness. Here are some key ways AI is influencing bug bounty hunting:

1. Vulnerability Scanning and Automation:

AI-powered vulnerability scanners can automatically crawl web applications and identify potential security issues, such as SQL injection, cross-site scripting (XSS), and more. This automation saves time for bug hunters and helps them focus on more complex tasks.

2. Behavior Analysis and Anomaly Detection:

AI algorithms can analyze user behavior and application interactions to identify potential anomalies that may indicate security risks or abnormal patterns.

3. Intelligent Fuzzing:

AI-powered fuzzing techniques can generate and test a vast range of inputs to identify unknown vulnerabilities, especially in complex software systems and APIs.

4. Exploit Generation and Validation:

AI models can assist in generating proof-of-concept exploits for identified vulnerabilities, validating their impact, and helping researchers demonstrate the severity to organizations.

5. Contextual Prioritization:

AI can analyze and prioritize vulnerabilities based on their severity, potential impact, and relevance to the organization's infrastructure. This allows researchers to focus on the most critical issues first.

6. Automated Response and Remediation:

AI-powered security solutions can automatically respond to certain types of attacks, block malicious traffic, and initiate remediation efforts, reducing the window of exposure.

7. Code Analysis and Pattern Recognition:

AI can analyze source code to identify patterns associated with known vulnerabilities and detect potentially risky code structures.

8. Security Testing in IoT and OT Devices:

AI is being used to simulate attacks on Internet of Things (IoT) and Operational Technology (OT) devices to identify vulnerabilities unique to these environments.

9. Adversarial AI Techniques:

Ethical hackers are exploring adversarial AI techniques to assess the resilience of AI-based security systems and to identify vulnerabilities in AI models.

10. Data Analysis for Threat Intelligence:

- AI can analyze vast amounts of threat intelligence data to identify emerging attack patterns, trends, and previously unseen vulnerabilities.

11. AI in Password Cracking and Brute-Force Attacks:

- AI-powered password cracking tools can improve the efficiency and success rate of brute-force attacks, highlighting the importance of strong password policies.

12. AI for Behavior-Based User Authentication:

- AI models can analyze user behavior patterns for context-based authentication and to detect anomalous login attempts.

AI is not replacing human bug hunters but rather enhancing their capabilities. Human expertise and intuition remain vital in finding complex and creative vulnerabilities that AI might miss. The collaboration between AI and human researchers is leading to more robust bug bounty hunting programs and helping organizations stay one step ahead of evolving cybersecurity threats.

12.4 Ethical Hacking's Role in Shaping Cyber Security's Future

Ethical hacking plays a crucial role in shaping the future of cybersecurity by actively contributing to identifying and mitigating vulnerabilities and enhancing overall security practices. Here are some key ways ethical hacking influences the future of cybersecurity:

1. Proactive Security Approach:

Ethical hacking promotes a proactive security approach, where organizations actively seek vulnerabilities before malicious actors can exploit them. By adopting this mindset, cybersecurity becomes more preventive rather than solely reactive.

2. Identifying Emerging Threats:

Ethical hackers continuously explore emerging technologies and trends to identify potential security risks and vulnerabilities. Their findings help the cybersecurity community prepare for new threats.

3. Improving Security Posture:

Through vulnerability assessments, penetration testing, and bug bounties, ethical hackers help organizations identify and address weaknesses in their systems, thereby improving their security posture.

4. Building Secure Software and Systems:

Ethical hackers' insights contribute to secure software development practices. By identifying and rectifying vulnerabilities during the development phase, security can be ingrained into the system's foundation.

5. Enhancing Incident Response and Recovery:

Ethical hackers' contributions help organizations better understand attack vectors and develop robust incident response and recovery plans to minimize the impact of security breaches.

6. Fostering Security Collaboration:

Ethical hacking promotes collaboration between security researchers, organizations, and the cybersecurity community. This collective effort leads to shared knowledge, best practices, and the ability to respond effectively to cyber threats.

7. Advancing Security Research:

Ethical hackers contribute to security research by discovering new attack vectors, analyzing emerging technologies, and developing novel techniques to defend against cyber threats.

8. Validating Security Investments:

Organizations invest significant resources in security technologies and solutions. Ethical hackers help validate the effectiveness of these investments by identifying vulnerabilities that might have been overlooked.

9. Encouraging Responsible Disclosure:

Ethical hackers adhere to responsible disclosure practices, giving organizations the opportunity to address vulnerabilities before they are exploited by malicious actors.

10. Driving Policy and Regulation:

- Ethical hackers' findings often shed light on cybersecurity gaps and vulnerabilities. These insights can influence policy decisions and lead to improved cybersecurity regulations and standards.

11. Bridging the Skills Gap:

- The demand for cybersecurity professionals is growing rapidly. Ethical hacking showcases the importance of cybersecurity expertise and can inspire individuals to pursue careers in the field.

12. Shaping Cybersecurity Culture:

- Ethical hacking promotes a culture of security awareness, making cybersecurity a shared responsibility across organizations and individuals.

As cybersecurity continues to be a paramount concern in an increasingly interconnected world, ethical hacking will remain instrumental in shaping the future of cybersecurity. The collaboration between ethical hackers, security professionals, organizations, and the broader cybersecurity community will be essential in effectively countering ever-evolving cyber threats and building a more secure digital landscape.

Congratulations on completing **<u>Bug Bounty Unleashed: Mastering the Art of Ethical Hacking and Rewards!</u>"** Throughout this comprehensive guide, you have explored the dynamic world of ethical hacking and bug bounty hunting, gaining invaluable insights into the realm of cybersecurity.

From the very beginning, you delved into the essence of bug bounty programs and their significance in proactively securing digital systems. You honed your skills, preparing yourself for the challenges that lay ahead by building a strong foundation in cybersecurity, mastering programming languages, and creating a secure testing environment.

Throughout the journey, you embraced the hacker's mindset and learned the systematic approach to uncovering vulnerabilities ethically. You explored the various types of vulnerabilities and the methods employed to exploit them, equipping yourself with the tools to fortify digital defenses effectively.

Intriguing case studies and real-life experiences of successful bug bounty hunters provided valuable insights, enabling you to overcome challenges and learn from failures. As you dived deeper into specialized areas such as IoT, OT, cloud, and containerized environments, you became adept at securing the most cutting-edge technologies.

Effectively reporting bugs and understanding responsible disclosure became second nature to you, ensuring the seamless collaboration between ethical hackers and program owners in safeguarding online assets. You also navigated the legal considerations, becoming well-versed in the ethical boundaries of your actions.

As you advanced, you discovered strategies for maximizing bug bounty rewards and gaining recognition within the thriving bug bounty community. Negotiating bounties and establishing your reputation as a skilled ethical hacker became part of your arsenal.

Finally, you gazed into the future of bug bounty hunting, embracing emerging trends, and preparing to adapt to the ever-changing landscape of cybersecurity. As you concluded this journey, your passion for ethical hacking and commitment to making the digital world safer has undoubtedly flourished.

As you embark on your ethical hacking endeavors, remember that your newfound knowledge and skills come with great responsibility. The impact of your actions can resonate far beyond your immediate endeavors. Embrace the ethos of ethical hacking and contribute to a secure and resilient cyberspace.

Always remain curious, relentless in your pursuit of knowledge, and committed to continuous improvement. The bug bounty community is vibrant and supportive, and your potential to make a positive difference is boundless.

Thank you for being part of "Bug Bounty Unleashed: Mastering the Art of Ethical Hacking and Rewards." Your journey as an ethical hacker has just begun, and the opportunities for growth and contribution are limitless.

Happy hacking and may you continue to secure the digital world one bounty at a time!

Russell Yates

www.ingramcontent.com/pod-product-compliance
Lightning Source LLC
Chambersburg PA
CBHW070927260726
48661CB00003B/859